Riding the Waves: Managing Emotional Flooding and Its Mental Health Impact

By Joycelyn Johnson, LPCC-s, LMHC

Disclaimer: The information provided here is for educational and informational purposes only and is not intended as a substitute for professional mental health advice, diagnosis, or treatment. Although I strive to provide accurate and up-to-date information, this content **should not** be used as a replacement for individual consultation with a licensed mental health professional. If you or someone you know is experiencing a mental health crisis, please contact a qualified mental health provider, call emergency services, or reach out to a crisis hotline - 988.

PLEASE NOTE – PLEASE NOTE – PLEASE NOTE

I am not a traditional writer, but I am passionate about using technology to develop and share basic mental health concepts that are accessible to everyone. My goal is to introduce existing foundational ideas that can help people improve their mental health and support the well-being of those they care about. These resources are designed for anyone who wants to learn and grow on their mental health journey.

There is so much I didn't know growing up, and I believe my mother didn't know either — largely because she was in survival mode, especially during my key developmental stages. This lack of knowledge, while understandable, is something I find unacceptable. I believe that understanding must come before action.

The books and materials I create are just the beginning of a learning and healing journey. Once you are exposed to new knowledge, it's impossible to "un-know" it. A seed has been planted, and the growth of that seed depends on how it is nurtured and cared for. My hope is that these tools will plant seeds of awareness, healing, and growth, sparking change that can ripple outward to create healthier individuals, families, and communities.

TABLE OF CONTENTS

Introduction (p. 5)

Part 1: The Foundations of Emotional Flooding
Chapter 1 - The Anatomy of Emotional Flooding (p. 9)
Chapter 2 - Triggers of Emotional Flooding (p. 13)
Chapter 3 - Emotional Flooding Across Life Stages (p. 17)

Part 2: The Link Between Emotional Flooding and Mental Health
Chapter 4 - Emotional Flooding and Common Mental Health Disorders (p. 24)
Chapter 5 - Chronic Emotional Flooding (p. 27)
Chapter 6 -The Interpersonal Toll (p. 31)

Part 3: Recognizing and Understanding Emotional Flooding
Chapter 7 - The Signs and Symptoms of Emotional Flooding (p. 37)
Chapter 8 - Assessing Emotional Flooding in Yourself and Others (p. 40)
Chapter 9 - Cultural and Social Considerations (p. 44)

Part 4: Managing Emotional Flooding
Chapter 10 - Immediate Coping Strategies (p. 50)
Chapter 11 - Preventative Measures (p. 54)
Chapter 12 - Developing Emotional Regulation Skills (p. 58)
Chapter 13 - Seeking Professional Support (p. 62)

Part 5: Emotional Flooding in Context
Chapter 14 - Emotional Flooding in Relationships (p. 68)
Chapter 15 - Workplace Impacts (p. 73)
Chapter 16 - Emotional Flooding in Parenting (p. 79)

Part 6: Thriving Beyond Emotional Flooding
Chapter 17 - Healing from Past Flooding Experiences (p. 85)
Chapter 18 - Building a Supportive Network (p. 90)
Chapter 19 Living with Emotional Awareness (p. 95)

Bonus Chapter - Emotional Flooding and Compulsive Behaviors – A Comprehensive Perspective (p. 101)

Conclusion (p. 106)

Includes Note Page, Additional Resources & Other Titles

Introduction

What Is Emotional Flooding?

Emotional flooding is an intense psychological and physiological experience where emotions become overwhelming and all-consuming, often leaving individuals feeling out of control. It is characterized by an overload of emotions — whether fear, anger, sadness, or guilt — that can make it difficult to think clearly or respond effectively. Emotional flooding is not a sign of weakness but rather a natural response to internal or external stressors. Understanding how and why it happens is essential to gaining control over our mental health.

At its core, emotional flooding is rooted in the brain's survival mechanisms, particularly in the amygdala, which takes over logical thinking during moments of perceived threat. While this response is vital for immediate survival in dangerous situations, it can be maladaptive when triggered in everyday scenarios, such as conflicts, work stress, or personal challenges. Learning about emotional flooding provides a foundation for understanding our emotional responses and creating pathways to manage them effectively.

The Personal and Social Cost of Emotional Flooding
Emotional flooding can ripple through every aspect of life. Consider the story of Lisa, a young professional who experiences emotional overwhelm during workplace conflicts, leading her to withdraw from opportunities for growth. Or David, a father whose emotional flooding prevents him from effectively supporting his teenage son during tough conversations. These stories illustrate how emotional flooding can strain relationships, hinder communication, and impact personal and professional success.

On a societal level, emotional dysregulation often carries stigma. Those who experience it are frequently labeled as "overly sensitive" or "dramatic," discouraging individuals from seeking help. This stigma not only isolates people but also perpetuates misunderstandings about emotional health. By shedding light on emotional flooding, this book aims to foster empathy and reduce the shame surrounding it.

Purpose of the Book
The purpose of this book is to demystify emotional flooding and provide actionable tools for managing it. Whether you're someone who frequently experiences emotional flooding, a loved one seeking to support someone else, or a professional aiming to deepen your understanding, this book offers insights and strategies for navigating emotional overwhelm.

We'll begin by exploring the science of emotional flooding, including the role of the brain, nervous system, and survival responses. From there, we'll delve into the triggers and life stages that shape emotional flooding, providing a comprehensive understanding of why it happens. In subsequent chapters, we'll examine how emotional flooding connects to mental health conditions like anxiety, depression, and PTSD, while also addressing its long-term effects on relationships, work, and physical health.

This book also emphasizes practical solutions. You'll learn how to recognize the signs of emotional flooding in yourself and others, implement immediate coping strategies, and build preventative habits that foster emotional resilience. By the end, you'll have a deeper understanding of emotional flooding and the tools to turn emotional overwhelm into opportunities for growth, healing, and connection.

Emotional flooding is a challenge, but it is not insurmountable. With the right knowledge and strategies, you can navigate these overwhelming moments and thrive beyond them. This book is your guide to understanding and transforming emotional flooding into emotional strength and stability.

Part 1 - The Foundations of Emotional Flooding

Chapter 1: The Anatomy of Emotional Flooding - Emotional flooding occurs when the brain's emotional processing center, the amygdala, takes over in response to a perceived threat, a phenomenon known as an "amygdala hijack." This triggers the body's survival mechanisms, activating the nervous system and leading to fight, flight, freeze, or fawn responses. These automatic reactions are designed to protect us but can be disruptive when triggered by non-life-threatening situations. Understanding this process provides crucial insights into why emotional flooding feels so overwhelming and difficult to manage.

Chapter 2: Triggers of Emotional Flooding - Emotional flooding can be set off by both external and internal triggers. External triggers include stressful environments, unresolved trauma, or sensory overload, such as loud noises or chaotic surroundings. Internal triggers often stem from negative self-talk, deeply buried emotions, or unresolved internal conflicts. Recognizing and identifying these triggers is essential for managing emotional flooding effectively, as it allows individuals to anticipate and mitigate emotional overwhelm.

Chapter 3: Emotional Flooding Across Life Stages - The manifestation of emotional flooding varies across different stages of life. In children, it might appear as tantrums or extreme reactions due to their limited ability to regulate emotions. Teenagers often experience mood swings or risky behaviors as their brains continue to develop. Adults might face emotional flooding as disproportionate stress responses, while older adults may experience it due to cognitive changes or life transitions. Additionally, societal expectations and biological differences influence how emotional flooding is experienced and expressed by different genders. Recognizing these variations helps tailor strategies for managing emotional flooding at every stage of life.

This section lays the groundwork for understanding emotional flooding by exploring its biological basis, identifying its triggers, and examining its manifestation across life stages, setting the stage for deeper discussions on its impact and management.

Chapter 1: The Anatomy of Emotional Flooding

Emotional flooding is a phenomenon that many people experience, yet few truly understand. It occurs when the brain's emotional processing center, the amygdala, takes control in response to a perceived threat. This reaction, often referred to as an "amygdala hijack," triggers the body's survival mechanisms, initiating the fight, flight, freeze, or fawn responses. While these automatic reactions are evolutionarily designed to protect us from physical danger, they can become highly disruptive when activated by non-life-threatening situations, such as disagreements, criticism, or overwhelming tasks. To navigate these moments, it's essential to grasp the anatomy of emotional flooding.

The Role of the Amygdala

The amygdala is a small, almond-shaped structure located deep within the brain. It acts as a rapid-response system, scanning for potential threats and initiating a cascade of physiological changes when danger is detected. This process happens faster than the rational brain, or prefrontal cortex, can evaluate the situation, ensuring our survival in critical moments. For instance, if you suddenly encounter a growling dog, the amygdala springs into action, sending signals to the body to prepare for fight or flight before you consciously assess the situation.

However, the amygdala does not differentiate between physical threats and emotional stressors. A harsh comment from a colleague or a heated argument with a loved one can elicit the same intense reaction as a life-threatening event. This overgeneralization of threats is what makes emotional flooding so pervasive in modern life.

The Nervous System's Response

When the amygdala perceives a threat, it activates the autonomic nervous system, particularly the sympathetic branch. This triggers the release of stress hormones such as adrenaline and cortisol, which prepare the body for immediate action.

Common physiological responses include:
- Increased heart rate
- Rapid breathing
- Muscle tension
- Heightened alertness

These changes are meant to enhance our ability to react quickly. However, in situations where the threat is not physical, these responses can feel overwhelming and out of place. For example, during a heated argument, you might feel your heart pounding, palms sweating, and thoughts racing, even though you are not in physical danger.

Why Emotional Flooding Feels Overwhelming
Emotional flooding feels intense because it effectively shuts down the rational brain. When the amygdala hijacks control, the prefrontal cortex—responsible for reasoning, decision-making, and impulse control—takes a backseat. This explains why people often say or do things they later regret during emotionally charged moments. The ability to think clearly and assess the situation objectively is compromised, leaving us at the mercy of raw emotion.

Additionally, emotional flooding can create a feedback loop. The physical symptoms of stress can reinforce the perception of danger, escalating the emotional response further. This cycle can make it incredibly difficult to calm down and regain control once flooding has begun.

Breaking Down the Fight, Flight, Freeze, and Fawn Responses
1. **Fight:** This response manifests as anger, aggression, or a need to confront the perceived threat. In emotionally charged situations, this might look like yelling, arguing, or becoming defensive.
2. **Flight:** This involves withdrawing or escaping from the situation. It might manifest as walking away from a conflict, avoiding certain people, or procrastinating on tasks that feel overwhelming.

3. **Freeze:** This response is characterized by a sense of being stuck or paralyzed. You might feel unable to make decisions or take action, as though you are mentally or emotionally frozen.
4. **Fawn:** Often overlooked, this response involves people-pleasing or appeasing behaviors to diffuse the perceived threat. For example, excessively apologizing or agreeing with someone to avoid conflict.

Understanding the Triggers

Emotional flooding is not random; it is often tied to specific triggers that vary from person to person. These triggers can include:

- **Past trauma:** Unresolved experiences can heighten sensitivity to certain situations.
- **Unmet emotional needs:** Feelings of rejection, abandonment, or inadequacy can quickly escalate into emotional flooding.
- **Cognitive distortions:** Negative thought patterns, such as catastrophizing or mind-reading, can amplify the perception of threat.

Identifying your triggers is a crucial step in managing emotional flooding. By recognizing the situations or interactions that provoke strong emotional responses, you can begin to anticipate and mitigate their impact.

The Path to Understanding

Understanding the anatomy of emotional flooding provides a foundation for managing it effectively. Recognizing that these intense reactions are a natural part of how the brain functions—rather than a personal failing—can reduce feelings of shame or frustration. With this knowledge, you can begin to explore strategies to calm the amygdala, engage the rational brain, and regain control during emotionally charged moments.

In the chapters ahead, we will delve into practical techniques for recognizing, interrupting, and recovering from emotional flooding, empowering you to navigate these experiences with greater resilience and clarity.

Chapter 2: Triggers of Emotional Flooding

Emotional flooding doesn't occur in a vacuum; it is set off by triggers that can be either external or internal. These triggers activate the brain's alarm system, sending the amygdala into overdrive and initiating the cascade of emotional and physiological responses that define emotional flooding. Understanding these triggers is a critical step toward managing emotional overwhelm and reclaiming a sense of balance in difficult moments. By identifying what sets off these intense reactions, individuals can learn to anticipate, prepare for, and potentially prevent emotional flooding.

External Triggers

External triggers are stimuli or situations in the environment that provoke an emotional response. While these triggers can vary widely from person to person, some common categories include:

1. **Stressful Environments:** High-pressure situations, such as a demanding workplace, financial strain, or conflict within personal relationships, can heighten emotional sensitivity. Over time, chronic stress can lower the threshold for emotional flooding, making even minor stressors feel overwhelming.
2. **Unresolved Trauma:** Past traumatic experiences often leave emotional scars that can resurface when certain situations or stimuli act as reminders. For example, a loud noise might remind someone of a traumatic event, triggering an intense emotional and physical response.
3. **Sensory Overload:** Environments with excessive noise, bright lights, or chaotic activity can overwhelm the senses, making it difficult for the brain to process information calmly. This overload can lead to heightened emotional reactivity.

4. **Interpersonal Conflict:** Arguments, criticism, or feelings of rejection from others can serve as powerful external triggers. When unresolved tension exists in a relationship, even small disagreements can escalate quickly into emotional flooding.

Internal Triggers

While external stimuli are often more visible, internal triggers can be equally, if not more, potent. These arise from within and often stem from deeper emotional and psychological patterns.

1. **Negative Self-Talk:** The inner dialogue we have with ourselves can significantly impact our emotional state. Harsh self-criticism, catastrophizing, or imagining worst-case scenarios can amplify feelings of inadequacy or fear, triggering emotional flooding.
2. **Deeply Buried Emotions:** Suppressed feelings, such as grief, anger, or shame, can lie dormant until they are inadvertently activated by a situation or interaction. When these emotions resurface, they often do so with an intensity that can feel overwhelming.
3. **Unresolved Internal Conflicts:** Internal struggles, such as conflicting values or unacknowledged desires, create emotional tension. For example, feeling torn between wanting to please others and maintaining personal boundaries can lead to an inner tug-of-war that triggers flooding.
4. **Physical States:** The body's condition plays a significant role in emotional reactivity. Fatigue, hunger, or illness can lower resilience, making it easier for both internal and external triggers to provoke emotional flooding.

Recognizing Patterns in Triggers

One of the keys to managing emotional flooding is identifying patterns in what triggers it. Keeping a journal or log of moments when emotional flooding occurs can be a helpful tool. Over time, patterns often emerge, revealing the specific circumstances or thoughts that consistently lead to emotional overwhelm.

Questions to consider include:
- What was happening in the environment when I began to feel flooded?
- Were there specific interactions or events that preceded the flooding?
- What thoughts or emotions were present in the moments leading up to the episode?

The Interplay of External and Internal Triggers

It's important to note that external and internal triggers often interact. For example, a stressful meeting at work (external) might activate feelings of self-doubt (internal), creating a compounded effect. Recognizing how these elements reinforce one another can provide deeper insights into why emotional flooding occurs and how to break the cycle.

Mitigating Triggers

While it is impossible to eliminate all potential triggers, taking steps to minimize their impact can reduce the frequency and intensity of emotional flooding episodes. Strategies include:

1. **Creating Supportive Environments:** Surrounding yourself with calm and supportive people and environments can reduce external stressors.
2. **Building Self-Awareness:** Developing a deeper understanding of your emotional patterns can help you recognize triggers before they escalate.
3. **Practicing Self-Compassion:** Counteracting negative self-talk with kinder, more affirming thoughts can help neutralize internal triggers.
4. **Developing Coping Mechanisms:** Techniques such as mindfulness, deep breathing, or grounding exercises can help manage the immediate effects of a trigger and prevent flooding from taking over.

Moving Forward

Recognizing and identifying triggers is not just about avoiding emotional flooding — it is about gaining greater control over your emotional landscape. By understanding the specific factors that provoke overwhelming reactions, you can develop strategies to navigate them with resilience and clarity. The journey of managing emotional flooding begins with this essential awareness and paves the way for a calmer, more centered life.

Chapter 3: Emotional Flooding Across Life Stages

Emotional flooding—the overwhelming surge of emotions in response to perceived threats or stressors—affects individuals differently across various stages of life. Understanding these differences can provide valuable insights into how emotional regulation develops and how strategies for managing emotional flooding can be tailored to each stage. From the tantrums of childhood to the reflective emotional experiences of older adulthood, the manifestations of emotional flooding are shaped by biological, cognitive, and social factors.

Emotional Flooding in Childhood

In children, emotional flooding often manifests as tantrums, meltdowns, or extreme reactions. This is because young children have not yet developed the cognitive tools to regulate their emotions effectively. The prefrontal cortex, which is responsible for self-control and reasoning, is still in the early stages of development. As a result, the amygdala takes the lead in processing intense emotions, often resulting in overwhelming displays of frustration, sadness, or anger.

Key Triggers in Childhood:
- **Frustration:** Difficulty completing a task or communicating needs can quickly escalate into emotional flooding.
- **Overstimulation:** Bright lights, loud noises, or chaotic environments can overwhelm a child's sensory system.
- **Separation Anxiety:** Feelings of abandonment or fear of losing a caregiver can provoke intense emotional responses.

Strategies for Management:
- **Validation:** Acknowledging the child's feelings helps them feel understood and reduces the intensity of their reaction.
- **Soothing Techniques:** Techniques such as deep breathing, a calm voice, or physical comfort can help regulate the child's emotions.

- **Teaching Emotional Literacy:** Introducing children to concepts like "hangry," "sad," or "frustrated" helps them articulate their feelings instead of acting them out.

Emotional Flooding in Adolescence

Adolescents experience a unique form of emotional flooding due to rapid brain development and hormonal changes. The prefrontal cortex is still maturing, while the amygdala remains highly active, leading to heightened emotional reactivity. This stage is also marked by identity formation and increased sensitivity to peer influence, which can amplify emotional responses.

Key Triggers in Adolescence:

- **Social Dynamics:** Rejection, bullying, or conflict with peers can lead to intense emotional flooding.
- **Performance Pressure:** Academic expectations or extracurricular demands often trigger feelings of inadequacy or overwhelm.
- **Identity Challenges:** Struggles with self-image or fitting in can provoke emotional outbursts.

Strategies for Management:

- **Active Listening:** Providing a safe space for teens to express their emotions without judgment fosters trust and reduces flooding.
- **Encouraging Reflection:** Helping teens recognize patterns in their emotional responses can build self-awareness and regulation skills.
- **Setting Boundaries:** Clear but flexible boundaries offer structure and reduce uncertainty, which can be a source of flooding.

Emotional Flooding in Adulthood

For adults, emotional flooding often presents as disproportionate stress responses to everyday challenges. This stage of life is marked by complex responsibilities such as work, relationships, and parenting, all of which can contribute to emotional overwhelm. While adults typically have a fully developed prefrontal cortex, chronic stress or unresolved emotional issues can still trigger flooding.

Key Triggers in Adulthood:
- **Workplace Stress:** Deadlines, conflicts, or job insecurity can lead to heightened emotional responses.
- **Relationship Issues:** Arguments, miscommunication, or unmet expectations in personal relationships can provoke flooding.
- **Parenting Demands:** Balancing the needs of children with personal and professional responsibilities can become overwhelming.

Strategies for Management:
- **Stress Reduction Techniques:** Practices like mindfulness, exercise, or journaling can help prevent flooding.
- **Emotional Awareness:** Recognizing and addressing unresolved emotional issues reduces susceptibility to triggers.
- **Support Systems:** Leaning on friends, family, or therapists provides emotional relief and perspective.

Emotional Flooding in Older Adulthood

In older adulthood, emotional flooding can be influenced by cognitive changes, health challenges, or significant life transitions. Loss of independence, grief over the death of loved ones, or reflections on life's meaning can make emotional experiences particularly intense.

Key Triggers in Older Adulthood:
- **Health Issues:** Chronic illness or physical limitations can lead to feelings of frustration or helplessness.

- **Social Isolation:** Reduced social connections can heighten sensitivity to emotional triggers.
- **Life Transitions:** Retirement or moving into assisted living can provoke feelings of loss or uncertainty.

Strategies for Management:
- **Maintaining Connections:** Staying socially active reduces feelings of isolation and emotional flooding.
- **Engaging in Meaningful Activities:** Pursuits that provide a sense of purpose, such as volunteering or hobbies, can mitigate emotional overwhelm.
- **Professional Support:** Therapy or counseling can help navigate the emotional complexities of this life stage.

Gender Differences in Emotional Flooding

Societal expectations and biological factors contribute to gender differences in how emotional flooding is experienced and expressed. For example, men might suppress their emotions due to cultural norms, leading to delayed or explosive flooding. Women, on the other hand, may experience heightened emotional sensitivity due to hormonal changes associated with life stages such as pregnancy or menopause.

Strategies for Addressing Gender Differences:
- **Challenging Stereotypes:** Encouraging open expression of emotions in all genders fosters healthier emotional regulation.
- **Tailoring Support:** Recognizing individual needs rather than relying on gender norms ensures effective management strategies.

Understanding how emotional flooding manifests across life stages highlights the importance of tailored approaches to managing it. Whether it's helping a child articulate their feelings, guiding a teenager through social challenges, or supporting an older adult through life transitions, recognizing the unique triggers and strategies for each stage fosters resilience and emotional well-being.

This comprehensive awareness allows individuals and their support systems to navigate emotional flooding with greater empathy and effectiveness.

Part 2 - The Link Between Emotional Flooding and Mental Health

Chapter 4: Emotional Flooding and Common Mental Health Disorders - Emotional flooding is intricately linked to various mental health conditions, such as anxiety, depression, PTSD, and borderline personality disorder. It often acts as both a symptom and a contributing factor to these disorders. For instance, individuals with anxiety may experience emotional flooding as heightened worry or fear that feels unmanageable, while those with PTSD may relive traumatic events through overwhelming emotional flashbacks. In borderline personality disorder, emotional flooding exacerbates intense and rapidly shifting emotions, impacting relationships and self-perception. Understanding its dual role as both a symptom and a standalone issue is critical to addressing the root causes of emotional overwhelm.

Chapter 5: Chronic Emotional Flooding - When emotional flooding becomes chronic, it can have profound long-term effects on brain health and overall resilience. Prolonged exposure to overwhelming emotions can impair the brain's ability to regulate stress, potentially leading to changes in the prefrontal cortex and amygdala. Physically, chronic emotional flooding is associated with stress-related illnesses, such as cardiovascular issues, weakened immune function, and gastrointestinal problems. It also contributes to fatigue, burnout, and reduced overall well-being, emphasizing the importance of early intervention and ongoing self-care to prevent lasting damage.

Chapter 6: The Interpersonal Toll - Emotional flooding significantly impacts relationships, often leading to communication breakdowns and strained connections. When individuals are overwhelmed by emotions, they may lash out, withdraw, or struggle to articulate their needs, creating barriers in personal and professional relationships.

Over time, this can lead to social withdrawal and isolation, further deepening feelings of emotional overwhelm. By recognizing the interpersonal consequences of emotional flooding, individuals can begin to rebuild trust, improve communication, and strengthen their support networks.

This section highlights the far-reaching effects of emotional flooding on mental health, physical well-being, and interpersonal relationships. It underscores the importance of addressing emotional flooding to foster resilience, improve mental health outcomes, and repair social connections.

Chapter 4: Emotional Flooding and Common Mental Health Disorders

Emotional flooding is deeply intertwined with several mental health disorders, playing a complex role as both a symptom and a contributing factor. It's overwhelming nature disrupts emotional regulation and intensifies the challenges faced by individuals with conditions such as anxiety, depression, PTSD, and borderline personality disorder. Understanding how emotional flooding interacts with these disorders is essential to providing effective support and treatment.

Anxiety Disorders and Emotional Flooding

For individuals with anxiety disorders, emotional flooding often manifests as an overwhelming cascade of worry and fear. The amygdala, hyper-alert to perceived threats, triggers a fight-or-flight response, even in situations that pose no real danger. This can lead to physical symptoms like a racing heart, shortness of breath, and sweating, compounding the emotional distress.

People with generalized anxiety disorder (GAD) may feel emotionally flooded by persistent concerns about daily life, while those with social anxiety might experience flooding during social interactions. In panic disorder, emotional flooding can occur suddenly, creating a sense of losing control or impending doom. Addressing these patterns involves grounding techniques and cognitive-behavioral strategies to reduce the amygdala's overactivity and build resilience against flooding episodes.

Depression and Emotional Flooding

In depression, emotional flooding often takes the form of despair, guilt, or hopelessness that feels inescapable. Negative self-talk and rumination amplify the emotional intensity, creating a cycle where individuals feel trapped in their thoughts and emotions. Unlike the heightened arousal of anxiety, emotional flooding in depression may feel heavy and immobilizing, leading to withdrawal and fatigue.

Recognizing the interplay between depression and emotional flooding is vital for treatment. Techniques such as mindfulness, reframing negative thoughts, and behavioral activation can help interrupt the flooding process and create space for emotional recovery.

Post-Traumatic Stress Disorder (PTSD)
Emotional flooding is a hallmark of PTSD, where individuals relive traumatic events through flashbacks, nightmares, or intrusive thoughts. These experiences are often accompanied by intense emotional and physical responses, such as terror, anger, or helplessness. The amygdala remains in a state of hypervigilance, reacting strongly to triggers that may not be immediately apparent.

Managing emotional flooding in PTSD requires addressing both the trauma and its triggers. Eye Movement Desensitization and Reprocessing (EMDR), trauma-focused therapy, and grounding exercises are effective in reducing the frequency and intensity of flooding episodes. Building a sense of safety and control is paramount to healing.

Borderline Personality Disorder (BPD)
In borderline personality disorder, emotional flooding exacerbates the emotional instability that defines the condition. Intense feelings of abandonment, anger, or shame can quickly spiral out of control, leading to impulsive actions or strained relationships. The heightened sensitivity of the amygdala plays a central role, making it difficult for individuals with BPD to regulate their emotions.

Dialectical behavior therapy (DBT) is particularly effective in helping individuals with BPD manage emotional flooding. Skills such as distress tolerance, emotional regulation, and interpersonal effectiveness enable individuals to navigate their emotions more constructively and reduce the impact of flooding on their lives.

Emotional Flooding as a Standalone Issue

While emotional flooding is often a symptom of these disorders, it can also occur independently, especially during periods of high stress or significant life changes. Understanding its standalone nature is critical for individuals who may not meet the criteria for a specific mental health diagnosis but still struggle with overwhelming emotions.

Addressing the Root Causes of Emotional Flooding

Managing emotional flooding involves a multifaceted approach that includes identifying triggers, building emotional resilience, and addressing any underlying mental health conditions. Techniques such as mindfulness, grounding, and therapy provide valuable tools for reducing emotional overwhelm. By understanding the dual role of emotional flooding as both a symptom and an independent challenge, individuals can gain the insights and support they need to navigate their emotional landscape effectively.

Emotional flooding is not an insurmountable challenge — it is a call to understand, adapt, and heal.

Chapter 5: Chronic Emotional Flooding

Emotional flooding, while often experienced as a temporary and situational response, can evolve into a chronic condition when it occurs frequently or remains unresolved. Chronic emotional flooding has profound implications for both mental and physical health, leading to lasting changes in brain function, increased vulnerability to illness, and diminished overall resilience. Understanding the effects of chronic emotional flooding highlights the critical need for early intervention and sustained self-care to mitigate long-term consequences.

The Neurological Impact of Chronic Emotional Flooding
When emotional flooding becomes a regular occurrence, the brain's ability to regulate stress can be significantly impaired. The repeated activation of the amygdala, the brain's emotional processing center, creates a heightened state of alertness that can interfere with normal functioning.

Key Neurological Changes:
- **Amygdala Overactivity:** Chronic flooding keeps the amygdala in a state of hypervigilance, increasing sensitivity to stress and emotional triggers.
- **Prefrontal Cortex Suppression:** The rational part of the brain, the prefrontal cortex, becomes less effective in regulating emotions and decision-making. This can lead to difficulties in problem-solving, impulse control, and maintaining emotional balance.
- **Hippocampal Shrinkage:** Chronic stress and flooding can shrink the hippocampus, the brain region involved in memory and learning, leading to difficulties in retaining information and recalling past events.

These changes not only perpetuate the cycle of emotional flooding but also reduce the brain's resilience, making it harder to recover from future episodes of emotional overwhelm.

Physical Consequences of Chronic Emotional Flooding
The body's stress response, while adaptive in short bursts, becomes harmful when activated continuously. Chronic emotional flooding keeps the autonomic nervous system — particularly the sympathetic branch — in overdrive, leading to a host of physical health issues.

Common Health Effects:
1. **Cardiovascular Problems:** Prolonged stress increases blood pressure and heart rate, raising the risk of heart disease and stroke.
2. **Weakened Immune Function:** Chronic flooding suppresses the immune system, making the body more susceptible to infections and illnesses.
3. **Gastrointestinal Issues:** Stress can disrupt digestion, leading to problems such as irritable bowel syndrome (IBS), ulcers, or chronic stomach discomfort.
4. **Fatigue and Burnout:** The constant activation of stress hormones depletes the body's energy reserves, causing persistent fatigue and burnout.

Emotional and Psychological Effects
The psychological toll of chronic emotional flooding can be just as debilitating as its physical effects. Over time, individuals may experience:

- **Increased Anxiety:** A heightened state of alertness can make it difficult to relax or feel safe, contributing to generalized anxiety.
- **Depression:** The sense of being overwhelmed and unable to cope can lead to feelings of hopelessness and despair.
- **Reduced Self-Efficacy:** Chronic flooding erodes confidence in one's ability to manage emotions, creating a sense of helplessness.
- **Relationship Strain:** Emotional flooding often spills over into interactions with others, leading to misunderstandings, conflict, or withdrawal from social connections.

Breaking the Cycle of Chronic Emotional Flooding
While chronic emotional flooding can feel insurmountable, targeted strategies can help break the cycle and restore balance. Early intervention and ongoing self-care are essential for mitigating its effects and promoting long-term well-being.

Key Strategies for Recovery

1. **Stress Reduction Practices:**
   - Techniques such as mindfulness, yoga, or progressive muscle relaxation can help calm the nervous system and reduce the intensity of emotional flooding.
2. **Cognitive Restructuring:**
   - Challenging and reframing negative thought patterns can shift perceptions of stress and reduce emotional overwhelm.
3. **Physical Self-Care:**
   - Regular exercise, a healthy diet, and adequate sleep support the body's resilience to stress and improve overall well-being.
4. **Therapeutic Support:**
   - Therapy modalities such as cognitive-behavioral therapy (CBT) or trauma-focused approaches can address underlying issues and build emotional regulation skills.
5. **Building Resilience:**
   - Developing coping mechanisms, such as problem-solving skills and emotional awareness, strengthens the brain's ability to recover from stress.

Preventing Chronic Emotional Flooding
Prevention is the most effective strategy for managing chronic emotional flooding. By addressing acute emotional flooding early and developing habits that promote emotional health, individuals can reduce the likelihood of long-term consequences.

Preventative Measures:
1. **Recognize Early Signs:** Identifying when emotional flooding is becoming frequent or unmanageable is the first step in preventing chronicity.
2. **Set Boundaries:** Learning to say no and prioritizing self-care can reduce exposure to overwhelming situations.
3. **Develop Support Networks:** Leaning on friends, family, or support groups provides a buffer against emotional overwhelm.

Conclusion

Chronic emotional flooding has far-reaching effects on the brain, body, and emotional well-being. However, with awareness, intervention, and a commitment to self-care, it is possible to break the cycle and rebuild resilience. By taking proactive steps to address emotional flooding and its triggers, individuals can reclaim control over their emotions and lead healthier, more balanced lives.

Chapter 6: The Interpersonal Toll

Emotional flooding doesn't only affect the individual experiencing it—its ripple effects often extend to personal and professional relationships. The inability to manage overwhelming emotions can lead to communication breakdowns, strained connections, and misunderstandings. Over time, these issues can erode trust and intimacy, fostering social withdrawal and isolation. Recognizing the interpersonal toll of emotional flooding is a crucial step in healing and rebuilding meaningful relationships.

How Emotional Flooding Impacts Communication

Effective communication relies on clarity, empathy, and active listening, all of which become compromised during episodes of emotional flooding. When emotions take over, the ability to articulate needs, understand others, or resolve conflicts diminishes.

Common Communication Challenges:

- **Lashing Out:** Intense emotions can lead to yelling, blaming, or criticizing, which may damage trust and escalate conflicts.
- **Withdrawing:** Some individuals respond to emotional flooding by shutting down or avoiding conversations, leaving issues unresolved.
- **Misinterpretation:** Overwhelmed by their own emotions, individuals may misread others' intentions, leading to unnecessary conflict or defensiveness.

These patterns not only hinder resolution in the moment but can also create long-term resentment and disconnection if left unaddressed.

Emotional Flooding in Personal Relationships

In close relationships, such as those with partners, family, or friends, emotional flooding can have a profound impact. Intense emotional responses may be perceived as unpredictable or unfair, leading to feelings of frustration or hurt in the other party.

Effects on Personal Relationships:

1. **Erosion of Trust:** Repeated episodes of emotional flooding can make others feel unsafe or uncertain about how to engage with the individual.
2. **Reduced Intimacy:** Emotional withdrawal or heightened defensiveness can create barriers to emotional closeness and vulnerability.
3. **Cycle of Reactivity:** In relationships, one partner's emotional flooding can trigger a reactive response in the other, creating a feedback loop of escalating emotions.

Emotional Flooding in Professional Settings

While professional relationships may not have the same depth as personal ones, they still require effective communication and emotional regulation. Emotional flooding in the workplace can lead to strained team dynamics, reduced productivity, and even career setbacks.

Workplace Challenges:

- **Conflict with Colleagues:** Emotional flooding can lead to outbursts or passive-aggressive behavior that undermines teamwork.
- **Difficulty Managing Feedback:** Overwhelming emotions may cause individuals to perceive constructive criticism as personal attacks.
- **Burnout:** Chronic emotional flooding can diminish an individual's capacity to manage workplace stress, contributing to exhaustion and disengagement.

The Social Withdrawal Trap

One of the most damaging interpersonal consequences of emotional flooding is the tendency toward social withdrawal. Feeling overwhelmed and misunderstood, individuals may isolate themselves, cutting off the very support networks that could help them recover. Over time, this isolation reinforces feelings of loneliness and emotional overwhelm, creating a self-perpetuating cycle.

Rebuilding Relationships Affected by Emotional Flooding

Healing the interpersonal toll of emotional flooding requires intentional effort and vulnerability. By addressing the underlying causes of flooding and developing healthier communication habits, individuals can begin to repair and strengthen their relationships.

Strategies for Rebuilding Relationships:

1. **Practice Emotional Regulation:** Techniques such as mindfulness, deep breathing, and grounding can help reduce the intensity of emotional flooding, making it easier to engage in constructive communication.
2. **Acknowledge the Impact:** Taking responsibility for how emotional flooding has affected others is a crucial step in rebuilding trust and demonstrating a commitment to change.
3. **Improve Communication Skills:** Learning to articulate needs calmly, listen actively, and approach conflicts with empathy can prevent misunderstandings and foster connection.
4. **Seek Support:** Couples or family therapy can provide a safe space to address patterns of emotional flooding and their impact on relationships.
5. **Set Boundaries:** Clear boundaries can reduce triggers and create a sense of safety for both the individual experiencing flooding and their loved ones.

Strengthening Support Networks

Strong support networks play a vital role in mitigating the interpersonal toll of emotional flooding. Building and maintaining these networks requires consistent effort and mutual understanding.

Tips for Strengthening Support Networks:

- **Open Communication:** Regularly share feelings and needs with trusted individuals to create a foundation of mutual understanding.
- **Be Present:** Show appreciation and invest time in relationships to nurture connections.
- **Practice Reciprocity:** Offer support to others when they are struggling, reinforcing the give-and-take dynamic of healthy relationships.

Moving Forward

The interpersonal toll of emotional flooding is significant but not insurmountable. By recognizing its impact and taking proactive steps to address it, individuals can repair damaged relationships, foster deeper connections, and build resilience within their support systems. Emotional flooding doesn't have to define relationships; with effort and understanding, it can become an opportunity for growth and stronger bonds.

Part 3 - Recognizing and Understanding Emotional Flooding

Chapter 7: The Signs and Symptoms of Emotional Flooding - Emotional flooding manifests through a range of physical, cognitive, and emotional symptoms. Physical signs include a racing heart, sweating, and muscle tension, which signal the body's heightened state of alert. Cognitively, individuals may experience racing thoughts, difficulty concentrating, or decision paralysis, as their logical thinking becomes overwhelmed. Emotionally, flooding often presents as intense feelings of fear, anger, sadness, or shame that feel uncontrollable and disproportionate to the situation. Recognizing these signs is the first step in identifying and addressing emotional flooding effectively.

Chapter 8: Assessing Emotional Flooding in Yourself and Others - To better understand emotional flooding, self-assessment tools and reflection exercises can help individuals recognize patterns and triggers in their emotional responses. Observing emotional flooding in others, such as loved ones or colleagues, requires a compassionate approach, focusing on behavioral cues and changes in demeanor. By understanding how emotional flooding shows up in different people, individuals can offer appropriate support while also fostering awareness of their own experiences.

Chapter 9: Cultural and Social Considerations - Cultural norms and systemic factors play a significant role in how emotional flooding is experienced and expressed. Societal expectations about emotional expression, especially for marginalized groups, can create additional pressures that exacerbate emotional flooding. For example, cultural stigmas around emotional vulnerability or systemic discrimination may amplify emotional overwhelm. Recognizing these unique pressures helps individuals navigate their experiences with greater understanding and encourages more inclusive approaches to managing emotional flooding.

This section provides essential tools for identifying and understanding emotional flooding in both oneself and others while addressing the broader cultural and social contexts that influence these experiences. It lays the groundwork for building self-awareness and fostering empathy in relationships.

Chapter 7: The Signs and Symptoms of Emotional Flooding

Emotional flooding is an overwhelming state where emotions surge to a level that surpasses the mind's ability to process them rationally. This phenomenon can be triggered by conflict, trauma, or even everyday stressors. Understanding its signs and symptoms is essential for managing it effectively and fostering emotional resilience.

Physical Signs of Emotional Flooding
The body often responds to emotional flooding as if it is under immediate threat, activating the fight-or-flight response. Physical symptoms can include:

- **A Racing Heart**: The body pumps more blood to prepare for action, even when no physical threat is present.
- **Sweating**: A natural response to stress, sweating helps regulate body temperature, but it can also be a visible marker of anxiety.
- **Muscle Tension**: Chronic stress from emotional flooding can leave muscles tight and aching, a physical manifestation of psychological strain.

These physical signals are often the first noticeable indicators that something is amiss.

Cognitive Signs of Emotional Flooding
When emotional flooding takes hold, cognitive processes become impaired. This can manifest in several ways:

1. **Racing Thoughts**: The mind struggles to focus, bombarded by an endless stream of anxious or negative thoughts.
2. **Difficulty Concentrating**: Tasks that require attention and logical thinking become challenging, as the brain's emotional centers overpower its rational ones.
3. **Decision Paralysis**: The ability to make decisions can be compromised, as emotional flooding clouds judgment and creates confusion.

This cognitive disruption can prevent individuals from responding effectively to the situation, often exacerbating feelings of helplessness.

Emotional Symptoms of Flooding
On an emotional level, flooding is marked by intense, often uncontrollable feelings. Common experiences include:

- **Fear**: A primal emotion that signals danger, fear during flooding may feel irrational or out of proportion to the situation.
- **Anger**: Sudden, intense anger can emerge, sometimes without a clear trigger, leaving individuals feeling out of control.
- **Sadness or Shame**: Emotional flooding often intensifies feelings of inadequacy or regret, deepening emotional pain.

These emotions may feel overwhelming and difficult to regulate, further amplifying the cycle of distress.

Why Recognition Matters
Identifying these signs is the first and most critical step in addressing emotional flooding. Without awareness, individuals may misinterpret their symptoms as evidence of personal failure or weakness, which can lead to further emotional distress.

By becoming attuned to the physical, cognitive, and emotional manifestations of flooding, individuals can begin to implement strategies to manage it. Techniques such as mindfulness, deep breathing, or seeking support from a trusted individual can help counteract these overwhelming sensations.

Emotional flooding, while intense, is a manageable experience with the right tools and awareness. Recognizing its symptoms empowers individuals to interrupt the cycle and regain control, paving the way for healthier emotional responses and relationships.

Chapter 8: Assessing Emotional Flooding in Yourself and Others

Emotional flooding can be a perplexing and challenging experience, not just for the individual going through it, but also for those around them. Assessing emotional flooding requires self-awareness, a willingness to reflect, and the ability to observe others with compassion. By recognizing the signs and patterns in yourself and others, you can create pathways for understanding, support, and healing.

Assessing Emotional Flooding in Yourself
Self-assessment is an essential tool for identifying emotional flooding. It involves observing your own emotional patterns, physical responses, and triggers. The following methods can help:

1. Reflection Exercises
- **Journaling**: Write down situations where you felt emotionally overwhelmed. Note what happened, how you felt, and what you did in response. Over time, patterns may emerge that reveal your triggers and coping mechanisms.
- **Emotion Tracking**: Use a daily mood tracker to monitor shifts in your emotional state. Apps or simple charts can help you visualize patterns.
- **Mind-Body Awareness**: Pay attention to physical sensations, such as a racing heart or tight muscles, that often accompany emotional flooding.

2. Identifying Triggers
- **Past Experiences**: Reflect on whether certain situations remind you of past trauma or unresolved issues.
- **Environmental Factors**: Notice how noise, crowded spaces, or work pressures affect your emotional state.
- **Relational Dynamics**: Evaluate how interactions with specific individuals or types of conversations influence your feelings.

Understanding your triggers can help you anticipate and manage emotional flooding more effectively.

3. Using Self-Assessment Tools
- **Questionnaires**: Tools like the Emotional Regulation Questionnaire (ERQ) or self-created checklists can help gauge your emotional responses.
- **Rating Scales**: Rate your emotional intensity on a scale from 1 to 10 during stressful situations to measure when you might be approaching emotional flooding.

Assessing Emotional Flooding in Others
Recognizing emotional flooding in others requires sensitivity and a keen eye for changes in their behavior or demeanor. Keep in mind that emotional flooding manifests differently depending on the individual.

1. Behavioral Cues
Look for signs such as:
- Sudden withdrawal or shutting down
- Increased irritability or anger
- Difficulty concentrating or completing tasks
- Heightened emotional reactions, such as crying or snapping at others

These cues may indicate that someone is overwhelmed and struggling to process their emotions.

2. Changes in Communication
Notice shifts in how the person communicates:
- **Tone**: Is their tone sharper or more defensive than usual?
- **Content**: Are they repeating themselves, struggling to find words, or fixating on negative thoughts?
- **Nonverbal Cues**: Observe their body language, such as crossed arms, tense posture, or avoidance of eye contact.

These changes can provide valuable insight into their emotional state.

3. Compassionate Observation
When assessing emotional flooding in others, approach them with empathy:
- **Ask Open-Ended Questions**: "How are you feeling right now?" or "What's been on your mind?"
- **Reflect What You See**: Gently share your observations, such as, "You seem a bit tense—are you okay?"
- **Avoid Judging**: Focus on understanding rather than fixing their emotional state.

Supporting Emotional Awareness in Yourself and Others
Once you've assessed emotional flooding, the next step is fostering awareness and offering support.

For Yourself:
- Practice mindfulness to ground yourself in the present moment.
- Use relaxation techniques, such as deep breathing or progressive muscle relaxation.
- Set aside time for self-care to recharge and build resilience.

For Others:
- Create a safe space where they feel heard and supported.
- Encourage them to take breaks or step away from stressful situations.
- Offer practical help, like assisting with tasks or just being present with them.

Fostering Growth Through Awareness

Assessing emotional flooding is not just about identifying the signs but also about building awareness and strategies to manage it. By reflecting on your experiences and observing others with compassion, you can develop a deeper understanding of emotional regulation. This understanding not only helps you navigate your own challenges but also strengthens your relationships, creating a foundation for mutual growth and support.

Chapter 9: Cultural and Social Considerations

Emotional flooding is not a one-size-fits-all experience. Cultural norms, societal expectations, and systemic factors profoundly influence how individuals experience, express, and cope with emotional overwhelm. Recognizing these cultural and social dimensions is essential for fostering empathy, self-compassion, and inclusivity in addressing emotional flooding.

Cultural Norms and Emotional Expression

Cultural backgrounds shape how emotions are understood and expressed. For some cultures, emotional restraint is valued, while others encourage open and expressive displays of feelings. These cultural norms can significantly impact how individuals experience emotional flooding:

- **Emphasis on Emotional Restraint**: In cultures where stoicism and emotional control are prized, people may suppress signs of emotional flooding, leading to internalized stress and delayed coping responses.
- **Encouragement of Emotional Expression**: In cultures where emotions are freely expressed, emotional flooding may be more visibly recognized and acknowledged, creating opportunities for community support.

Understanding these cultural norms can help individuals and those around them interpret emotional flooding more effectively and avoid misjudgments.

Societal Expectations and Marginalized Groups

For marginalized communities, societal pressures and systemic inequities can exacerbate emotional flooding. These factors often intersect with cultural norms, adding layers of complexity to emotional experiences.

1. Stigma Around Emotional Vulnerability

- Marginalized groups may face stigmas about emotional expression, such as being perceived as "too emotional" or "weak." This can discourage people from seeking help or acknowledging their emotional flooding.
- For example, men in many cultures may be socialized to suppress vulnerability, while women may face stereotypes about being overly emotional, making it harder for either group to navigate emotional overwhelm openly.

2. Systemic Discrimination

- Experiencing systemic oppression, such as racism, sexism, or ableism, creates chronic stress that amplifies emotional flooding. Microaggressions, exclusion, and inequities can heighten emotional responses, often making them feel disproportionate to isolated incidents.
- For example, a person of color facing workplace discrimination may experience heightened emotional flooding due to the cumulative weight of previous inequities and invalidation.

3. Intersectionality

- People with overlapping marginalized identities—such as race, gender, socioeconomic status, or sexual orientation—may face compounded pressures that intensify emotional flooding. Recognizing this intersectionality is vital for understanding their unique emotional experiences.

Social Dynamics and Emotional Flooding

Social relationships and environments also shape how emotional flooding manifests:

1. Familial and Community Expectations

- Family and community expectations can either mitigate or exacerbate emotional flooding. For instance, close-knit communities may provide emotional support that buffers against flooding, while others may reinforce harmful norms that discourage emotional expression.

2. Workplace and Institutional Cultures

- Workplace dynamics and institutional cultures also play a role. High-pressure environments or those lacking psychological safety can create conditions where emotional flooding becomes frequent and debilitating.

3. Social Media and Comparison

- The rise of social media adds another layer of complexity. Constant comparison, exposure to distressing news, or online conflicts can contribute to emotional flooding in ways that were not present in earlier generations.

Strategies for Navigating Cultural and Social Pressures

Acknowledging these cultural and systemic influences is the first step toward creating inclusive strategies for managing emotional flooding:

1. Cultivating Cultural Sensitivity

- Develop an understanding of how cultural norms influence emotional expression. Recognizing that people cope differently based on their cultural upbringing helps avoid judgment and fosters deeper empathy.

2. Building Supportive Spaces
- Create environments where individuals feel safe expressing their emotions without fear of stigma. For marginalized groups, this might mean finding culturally affirming therapists, joining support groups, or cultivating relationships within their communities.

3. Challenging Systemic Barriers
- Advocate for systemic changes that reduce chronic stressors, such as policies promoting equity and inclusion in workplaces, schools, and other institutions.

4. Personal Reflection
- Reflect on how your own cultural background and societal context shape your emotional experiences. Recognizing biases and pressures allows for greater self-compassion and intentional emotional management.

Toward Inclusivity and Understanding
Understanding emotional flooding within cultural and social contexts enriches our ability to address it effectively. By acknowledging the unique pressures faced by individuals from diverse backgrounds, we can develop more empathetic and inclusive approaches to managing emotional overwhelm. This awareness not only improves individual coping but also fosters a collective effort toward equity and emotional well-being for all.

Part 4 - Managing Emotional Flooding

Chapter 10: Immediate Coping Strategies - When emotional flooding strikes, immediate coping strategies can help calm the mind and body. Grounding techniques — such as focusing on physical sensations, sensory inputs, or mindfulness practices — anchor individuals in the present moment, reducing emotional intensity. Breathing exercises, like deep diaphragmatic breathing or box breathing, are quick and effective methods to slow the heart rate and regain composure. These strategies provide relief in the moment, allowing individuals to regain control during overwhelming situations.

Chapter 11: Preventative Measures - Preventing emotional flooding requires proactive habits that build emotional resilience over time. Routine self-care practices, such as regular exercise, balanced nutrition, and sufficient sleep, strengthen the mind and body's ability to handle stress. Identifying and minimizing environmental and emotional triggers, whether through setting boundaries or reducing exposure to stressors, further reduces the likelihood of emotional flooding. These preventative measures create a foundation for long-term emotional stability.

Chapter 12: Developing Emotional Regulation Skills - Emotional regulation is a critical skill for managing emotional flooding effectively. Techniques from cognitive-behavioral therapy (CBT) help individuals reframe negative thought patterns and reduce cognitive distortions. Dialectical behavior therapy (DBT) emphasizes mindfulness, distress tolerance, and emotional intelligence, enabling individuals to navigate intense emotions with greater control. Developing these skills enhances emotional flexibility and fosters healthier responses to stress.

Chapter 13: Seeking Professional Support - For individuals struggling to manage emotional flooding on their own, professional support can be transformative. Therapy or counseling provides a safe space to explore underlying issues and develop tailored coping strategies.

In some cases, medication may play a role in stabilizing emotional responses, particularly for those with underlying mental health conditions. Recognizing when to seek professional help is an important step toward healing and resilience.

This section equips readers with a comprehensive toolkit for managing emotional flooding, from immediate relief techniques to preventative habits, emotional regulation skills, and professional support. Together, these strategies empower individuals to navigate and overcome emotional overwhelm effectively.

Chapter 10: Immediate Coping Strategies

When emotional flooding strikes, it can feel as though you are caught in a powerful current with no way out. The intensity of emotions can be overwhelming, but immediate coping strategies offer a lifeline, helping you calm your mind and body in the moment. These techniques focus on grounding, breathing, and mindfulness to regain control and create a sense of safety.

Grounding Techniques

Grounding techniques are designed to anchor you in the present moment, pulling your focus away from overwhelming emotions and back to the here and now. They engage your senses and physical sensations to interrupt the emotional surge.

1) 5-4-3-2-1 Method

This technique uses your senses to bring you back to the present:

- Identify **5 things you can see.**
- Identify **4 things you can touch.**
- Identify **3 things you can hear.**
- Identify **2 things you can smell.**
- Identify **1 thing you can taste.**

By focusing on your immediate surroundings, you can break the cycle of spiraling thoughts and reconnect with your environment.

2) Physical Grounding

Engage your body to redirect emotional energy:

- **Feel the ground beneath your feet:** Stand barefoot if possible and notice the texture and temperature of the surface.
- **Hold a cold or warm object:** Grasp a piece of ice or a warm mug and focus on the sensation in your hands.

- **Stretch or press your palms together:** Gentle physical activity can help release tension and provide a calming effect.

3) Mental Grounding
Use cognitive tasks to shift your focus:
- Recite the alphabet backward or name a category of objects (e.g., cities, animals).
- Repeat a calming mantra, such as "This too shall pass" or "I am safe."

Breathing Exercises
Breathing is one of the quickest and most effective ways to calm the nervous system during emotional flooding. Controlled breathing slows the heart rate, reduces muscle tension, and signals the brain that the body is safe.

1) Diaphragmatic Breathing
- Sit or lie down in a comfortable position.
- Place one hand on your chest and the other on your belly.
- Inhale deeply through your nose, letting your belly rise while keeping your chest still.
- Exhale slowly through your mouth, allowing your belly to fall.
- Repeat for several minutes, focusing on the rise and fall of your belly.

This technique promotes deep, steady breaths that activate the body's relaxation response.

2) Box Breathing
Box breathing is simple and structured:
- Inhale through your nose for a count of 4.
- Hold your breath for a count of 4.
- Exhale through your mouth for a count of 4.
- Hold your breath for another count of 4.
- Repeat the cycle as needed.

The rhythmic nature of box breathing can quickly bring a sense of calm and control.

3) 4-7-8 Breathing
This technique is particularly effective for reducing anxiety:
- Inhale through your nose for a count of 4.
- Hold your breath for a count of 7.
- Exhale through your mouth for a count of 8.
- Repeat 4 to 8 times.

The extended exhale helps slow the heart rate and lower stress levels.

Mindfulness Practices
Mindfulness is the practice of staying present and observing your thoughts and feelings without judgment. During emotional flooding, mindfulness can help you detach from the intensity of your emotions and view them as temporary experiences.

1. Body Scan
A body scan helps you identify and release physical tension:
- Sit or lie down comfortably.
- Close your eyes and take a few deep breaths.
- Focus on one part of your body at a time, starting with your toes and moving upward.
- Notice any tension or discomfort, and gently release it with each exhale.

2. Mindful Observation
Choose an object in your environment to focus on, such as a plant or a piece of jewelry:
- Observe its color, texture, shape, and any other details.
- Engage your senses fully and allow your thoughts to settle as you focus on the object.

3. Anchor in the Breath

Bring your awareness to your breath:

- Notice the sensation of air entering and leaving your nostrils.
- Pay attention to the rise and fall of your chest or belly.
- If your mind wanders, gently guide it back to your breath.

Mindfulness practices help you approach your emotions with curiosity and compassion, rather than fear or resistance.

Putting It All Together

When emotional flooding occurs, these strategies can be combined for maximum effect. For example, you might use diaphragmatic breathing alongside the 5-4-3-2-1 method or pair a body scan with box breathing. The key is to experiment and discover which techniques resonate most with you.

These immediate coping strategies provide relief in the moment, creating a space where you can regain control and composure. Over time, practicing these techniques can strengthen your ability to navigate emotional flooding with confidence and resilience.

Chapter 11: Preventative Measures

While immediate coping strategies can help manage emotional flooding in the moment, preventing it from occurring in the first place is an even more powerful approach. Preventative measures build emotional resilience and create a solid foundation for long-term emotional stability. By incorporating proactive habits into your daily routine and addressing potential triggers, you can reduce the likelihood of becoming emotionally overwhelmed.

The Power of Routine Self-Care

Routine self-care is the cornerstone of preventing emotional flooding. When the body and mind are well-nourished, rested, and active, they are better equipped to handle stress and maintain balance.

1. Regular Exercise

Physical activity is a natural stress reliever that strengthens the body's ability to manage emotional challenges:

- **Benefits**: Exercise reduces cortisol (the stress hormone), boosts endorphins, and improves mood.
- **Practical Tips**: Aim for 30 minutes of moderate exercise most days, whether it's walking, dancing, swimming, or yoga.

2. Balanced Nutrition

What you eat affects your emotional well-being:

- **Benefits**: A well-balanced diet stabilizes blood sugar, supports brain health, and prevents mood swings.
- **Practical Tips**: Incorporate whole foods, lean proteins, healthy fats, and complex carbohydrates into your meals. Minimize processed foods, caffeine, and excessive sugar.

3. Sufficient Sleep

Sleep is essential for emotional regulation and resilience:

- **Benefits**: Restful sleep restores cognitive function, reduces irritability, and increases stress tolerance.
- **Practical Tips**: Establish a consistent sleep routine, limit screen time before bed, and create a calming bedtime environment.

Identifying and Minimizing Triggers

Preventing emotional flooding also involves recognizing and reducing exposure to triggers that lead to overwhelm.

1. Identify Emotional and Environmental Triggers

Reflection: Consider situations, people, or environments that frequently cause emotional distress.

> **Examples**: Toxic relationships, excessive workload, or overstimulating environments.

2. Set Boundaries

Why It's Important: Clear boundaries protect your emotional well-being by preventing overcommitment and unnecessary stress.

> **Practical Tips**: Learn to say no to activities or requests that deplete your energy. Communicate your limits assertively and with compassion.

3. Reduce Exposure to Stressors

Evaluate Your Environment: Declutter your space, limit exposure to negative media, and create a calming home or work atmosphere.

> **Manage Relationships**: Surround yourself with supportive and understanding people. Minimize time spent with individuals who contribute to emotional distress.

Building Emotional Resilience

Emotional resilience is the ability to adapt and recover from stressful situations. Developing resilience helps prevent emotional flooding by making you more equipped to handle life's challenges.

1. Practice Mindfulness and Meditation

Why It's Effective: Mindfulness increases self-awareness and teaches you to respond to emotions with intention rather than reactivity.

Practical Tips: Dedicate a few minutes each day to mindfulness meditation, focusing on your breath or observing your thoughts without judgment.

2. Cultivate Healthy Coping Mechanisms

Examples: Journaling, creative outlets, and hobbies can provide an emotional release and help you process feelings constructively.

Practical Tips: Identify activities that bring you joy and relaxation, and incorporate them into your routine.

3. Strengthen Social Connections

Why It's Important: Supportive relationships buffer against stress and provide a safe space to share emotions.

Practical Tips: Make time to connect with loved ones regularly, whether through phone calls, shared meals, or community activities.

Long-Term Stress Management

Preventative measures also involve strategies to reduce overall stress levels and maintain emotional balance over time.

1. Time Management

Why It's Effective: Effective time management reduces the chaos that contributes to emotional flooding.

Practical Tips: Prioritize tasks, use tools like planners or digital calendars, and schedule downtime.

2. Therapeutic Practices

Options: Therapy or counseling can provide tools to manage emotional triggers and build resilience.

Practical Tips: Seek professional support when needed, whether for guidance, accountability, or addressing past trauma.

3. Engage in Regular Self-Reflection

Why It's Important: Reflecting on your experiences helps identify patterns and opportunities for growth.

Practical Tips: Set aside time each week to review your emotional responses, celebrate progress, and adjust strategies as needed.

Creating a Foundation for Stability

Preventing emotional flooding is not about eliminating stress or challenges from your life — it's about strengthening your capacity to handle them. By integrating self-care practices, minimizing triggers, and building resilience, you can create a foundation for emotional stability that supports you through life's ups and downs.

These preventative measures not only reduce the likelihood of emotional flooding but also enhance your overall well-being. With consistency and intention, you can foster a calmer, more balanced state of mind and a greater sense of control over your emotional health.

Chapter 12: Developing Emotional Regulation Skills

Emotional regulation is the ability to manage and respond to emotional experiences in a healthy and constructive way. For individuals prone to emotional flooding, strengthening this skill is crucial for maintaining control and fostering resilience. Techniques from evidence-based therapies such as Cognitive Behavioral Therapy (CBT) and Dialectical Behavior Therapy (DBT) offer practical tools to help reframe negative thoughts, build mindfulness, and develop emotional flexibility.

The Foundations of Emotional Regulation
Emotional regulation is not about suppressing emotions but about understanding, processing, and responding to them effectively. It involves:

- **Awareness**: Recognizing and naming emotions as they arise.
- **Understanding**: Identifying the triggers and patterns behind emotional reactions.
- **Management**: Employing strategies to reduce emotional intensity and maintain balance.

These foundations enable individuals to respond to challenges with greater composure and clarity.

Techniques from Cognitive Behavioral Therapy (CBT)
CBT focuses on the connection between thoughts, emotions, and behaviors. By identifying and challenging negative thought patterns, individuals can reduce the intensity of emotional flooding.

1. Cognitive Reframing
Reframing involves identifying distorted or negative thoughts and replacing them with more balanced perspectives.

> **Example**: Replace "I'll never get through this" with "This is challenging, but I can handle it step by step."

Practical Tips:
- Write down the triggering thought.
- Ask yourself: Is this thought based on facts, or is it an assumption?
- Generate alternative, more constructive thoughts.

2. Challenging Cognitive Distortions
Common cognitive distortions, such as catastrophizing or black-and-white thinking, fuel emotional flooding.

Example: Instead of thinking, "Everything is ruined," try, "Some things didn't go as planned, but there's still room to improve."

Practical Tips:
- Identify patterns of distorted thinking.
- Use logic and evidence to challenge these thoughts.
- Practice self-compassion when evaluating your reactions.

3. Behavioral Activation
Engaging in positive activities can interrupt cycles of negative thinking and emotional overwhelm.

Practical Tips:
- Create a list of enjoyable or meaningful activities.
- Schedule one activity each day, even when you don't feel like it.

Techniques from Dialectical Behavior Therapy (DBT)
DBT integrates mindfulness, distress tolerance, and emotional intelligence to help individuals navigate intense emotions with greater control.

1. Mindfulness Practices
Mindfulness helps individuals stay present and observe emotions without judgment.

Practical Tips:

- Practice mindful breathing: Focus on the sensation of your breath entering and leaving your body.
- Use the "What" and "How" skills of mindfulness:
  o **What**: Observe, describe, and participate in the moment.
  o **How**: Be nonjudgmental, focus on one thing at a time, and do what works for the situation.

2. Distress Tolerance Skills
These skills help manage emotional crises without making the situation worse.

Examples:
- **TIPP**: Use temperature (e.g., a cold pack), intense exercise, paced breathing, and progressive muscle relaxation to calm the body quickly.
- **STOP**: Stop, take a step back, observe the situation, and proceed mindfully to avoid impulsive reactions.

3. Building Emotional Intelligence
DBT emphasizes understanding and working with emotions, rather than against them.

Practical Tips:
- Keep an emotion diary: Track what you feel, the triggers, and how you responded.
- Learn to identify secondary emotions (e.g., shame about feeling angry) and focus on addressing the primary emotion.

Enhancing Emotional Flexibility
Emotional flexibility refers to the ability to adapt to changing emotional experiences. Developing this skill reduces the likelihood of emotional flooding and fosters healthier responses to stress.

1. Practice Self-Compassion

Be kind to yourself when you experience emotional flooding. Remind yourself that emotions are natural and that struggling doesn't mean failure.

Example: Replace self-criticism with supportive statements, such as, "It's okay to feel this way. I'm doing my best."

2. Develop a Toolbox of Coping Skills

Not every situation requires the same approach. Build a variety of coping strategies to handle different emotional challenges.

Examples: Breathing exercises, journaling, talking to a trusted friend, or engaging in creative activities.

3. Strengthen Problem-Solving Skills

Many emotional reactions stem from unresolved problems. Learning to address issues proactively can reduce stress and prevent flooding.

Practical Tips:
- Identify the problem clearly.
- Brainstorm possible solutions.
- Choose one solution to try and evaluate its effectiveness.

Putting Emotional Regulation Skills into Practice

Developing emotional regulation skills takes time and consistent effort. Begin by practicing one or two techniques that resonate with you, and gradually expand your toolkit. Over time, these skills will become second nature, allowing you to navigate intense emotions with greater confidence and control.

By integrating techniques from CBT and DBT, you can enhance your emotional flexibility, reduce the likelihood of flooding, and respond to stress in healthier, more constructive ways. Emotional regulation is not just a skill—it's a lifelong practice that empowers you to face life's challenges with grace and resilience.

Chapter 13: Seeking Professional Support

Managing emotional flooding can feel overwhelming, especially when it persists despite efforts to cope. For many individuals, seeking professional support is a transformative step toward understanding and managing their emotions. Therapists, counselors, and medical professionals offer tailored strategies and interventions that address the root causes of emotional flooding, providing tools for healing and long-term resilience.

The Role of Therapy in Managing Emotional Flooding
Therapy or counseling provides a structured and supportive environment for individuals to explore their emotions, identify triggers, and develop effective coping strategies.

1. Creating a Safe Space
- **What to Expect**: A trained therapist provides a nonjudgmental, confidential space where you can openly discuss your experiences.
- **Benefits**: Sharing your emotions and experiences with a professional can validate your feelings and reduce the sense of isolation that often accompanies emotional flooding.

2. Exploring Underlying Issues
- Emotional flooding is often rooted in unresolved issues, such as past trauma, chronic stress, or relationship difficulties.
- Therapists use evidence-based techniques to uncover and address these underlying factors, promoting deeper healing.

3. Learning Tailored Coping Strategies
- Therapists help individuals identify coping mechanisms that work best for their unique situations.
- Techniques may include cognitive restructuring, mindfulness practices, and distress tolerance skills.

Types of Therapy for Emotional Flooding:
- **Cognitive Behavioral Therapy (CBT)**: Focuses on identifying and reframing negative thought patterns.
- **Dialectical Behavior Therapy (DBT)**: Teaches mindfulness, emotional regulation, and distress tolerance skills.
- **Trauma-Focused Therapy**: Helps individuals process and heal from past traumatic experiences that may contribute to emotional flooding.

When Medication May Be Beneficial

In some cases, emotional flooding may be linked to underlying mental health conditions, such as anxiety disorders, depression, or post-traumatic stress disorder (PTSD). Medication can be a helpful tool in stabilizing emotional responses and improving overall well-being.

1. Understanding Medication's Role
- Medication is not a cure-all but can provide relief from symptoms, allowing individuals to engage more effectively in therapy and daily life.

2. Common Medications for Emotional Regulation
- **Antidepressants**: May help regulate mood and reduce emotional reactivity.
- **Anxiolytics**: Can alleviate acute anxiety that exacerbates emotional flooding.
- **Mood Stabilizers**: Useful for conditions such as bipolar disorder, where intense emotional swings are common.

3. Working with a Psychiatrist
- If medication is recommended, a psychiatrist will assess your needs and develop a treatment plan.
- Regular follow-ups ensure the medication is effective and adjusted as needed.

Recognizing When to Seek Professional Help

It's not always easy to know when to seek professional support. However, certain signs indicate that external help may be necessary:

1. Persistent Emotional Flooding
- If emotional flooding occurs frequently or feels unmanageable despite using coping strategies, professional support can provide relief.

2. Impact on Daily Life
- Emotional flooding that interferes with work, relationships, or daily functioning is a strong signal to seek help.

3. Co-occurring Mental Health Concerns
- If emotional flooding is accompanied by symptoms of anxiety, depression, or trauma, a therapist or psychiatrist can address these conditions holistically.

4. Feelings of Hopelessness
- Persistent feelings of hopelessness or thoughts of self-harm are serious indicators that professional intervention is needed immediately.

How to Begin the Process

1. Identify Your Needs
- Determine whether you're looking for therapy, medication, or both.
- Reflect on whether you'd prefer in-person sessions or virtual options.

2. Find a Qualified Professional
- Look for licensed therapists, counselors, or psychiatrists with experience in managing emotional flooding or related concerns.
- Consider asking for recommendations from trusted friends, family members, or healthcare providers.

3. Prepare for the First Session
- Be ready to discuss your experiences, triggers, and goals for therapy.
- Remember, the first session is an opportunity to assess whether the professional is a good fit for your needs.

The Benefits of Professional Support
Seeking professional support is a courageous step that can lead to profound personal growth. It not only helps manage emotional flooding but also builds skills and insights that improve overall emotional well-being. Benefits include:

- **Increased Self-Awareness**: Therapy fosters a deeper understanding of your emotional responses and triggers.
- **Enhanced Coping Skills**: You'll learn strategies tailored to your unique experiences and challenges.
- **Improved Relationships**: By managing emotional flooding, you can communicate more effectively and maintain healthier connections with others.
- **Long-Term Resilience**: Therapy equips you with tools to handle future stressors, reducing the risk of emotional flooding over time.

A Path Toward Healing and Resilience
Emotional flooding can feel like an insurmountable challenge, but professional support offers a pathway to healing and resilience. Whether through therapy, medication, or a combination of approaches, individuals can gain the tools they need to navigate intense emotions and build a more balanced and fulfilling life.

Recognizing the need for help is not a sign of weakness—it is a powerful step toward reclaiming control and investing in your emotional health. With the guidance of a professional, you can move from feeling overwhelmed to feeling empowered, one step at a time.

Part 5 - Emotional Flooding in Context

Chapter 14: Emotional Flooding in Relationships - Emotional flooding can significantly disrupt communication, intimacy, and trust within relationships. Overwhelmed by intense emotions, individuals may lash out, withdraw, or struggle to articulate their feelings, leading to misunderstandings and conflict. To navigate these challenges, partners and family members can employ strategies such as active listening, creating space for emotional processing, and offering empathetic support. Building mutual understanding and developing shared techniques for managing emotional flooding strengthens relationships and fosters emotional connection.

Chapter 15: Workplace Impacts - In high-pressure work environments, emotional flooding can hinder performance, decision-making, and workplace relationships. Employees may experience overwhelm in response to stress, conflict, or demanding tasks, while employers might struggle to address emotional needs effectively. Strategies for navigating emotional flooding in the workplace include fostering open communication, offering mindfulness training, and creating policies that promote emotional safety. Employers can further support employees by providing access to resources like counseling or stress management programs, ensuring a healthier and more productive work environment.

Chapter 16: Emotional Flooding in Parenting - Parenting introduces unique challenges when emotional flooding arises in both parents and children. Recognizing emotional flooding in children and teens is critical, as they may struggle to articulate their feelings and instead act out or withdraw. Parents can manage these situations by modeling healthy emotional regulation, creating a safe space for children to express their emotions, and teaching coping strategies like breathing exercises or mindfulness. By fostering emotional resilience within the family, parents help their children build lifelong skills for managing overwhelm.

This section explores how emotional flooding manifests in various contexts—relationships, workplaces, and parenting—highlighting its unique challenges and providing actionable strategies to navigate emotional overwhelm effectively in each setting.

Chapter 14: Emotional Flooding in Relationships

Emotional flooding doesn't just affect individuals — it ripples outward, influencing how people interact and connect with those closest to them. In relationships, whether romantic, familial, or platonic, emotional flooding can create barriers to communication, intimacy, and trust. When one or both parties are overwhelmed by intense emotions, conflicts may escalate, misunderstandings deepen, and emotional distance grow. However, with awareness and intentional strategies, it is possible to navigate these challenges and build stronger, more resilient connections.

How Emotional Flooding Disrupts Relationships

Emotional flooding often manifests in ways that strain relationships. Understanding its impact is the first step toward addressing it effectively.

1. Breakdowns in Communication

When emotions run high, logical thinking often takes a backseat. This can lead to:

- **Lashing Out**: Expressing frustration or anger in hurtful ways.
- **Shutting Down**: Withdrawing from conversations or avoiding the issue altogether.
- **Miscommunication**: Struggling to articulate feelings clearly, leading to misunderstandings.

2. Erosion of Trust and Intimacy

- Emotional flooding can make individuals feel unsafe, unheard, or invalidated in the relationship.
- Repeated conflicts may create emotional distance.
- Overwhelmed partners may feel unsupported or misunderstood.

3. Escalation of Conflict

- Emotional flooding often leads to reactive behavior, escalating minor disagreements into significant conflicts.

- Power struggles or blame games can overshadow problem-solving efforts.
- Emotional reactivity may prevent resolution, leaving issues unresolved.

Recognizing Emotional Flooding in Relationships

Recognizing the signs of emotional flooding in yourself and your partner is critical for addressing it constructively.

Signs in Yourself:
1. Feeling overwhelmed, irritable, or defensive during a conversation.
2. Experiencing a racing heart, sweaty palms, or shallow breathing.
3. Finding it hard to focus on what the other person is saying.

Signs in Your Partner:
1. Raised voice, aggressive tone, or sudden withdrawal.
2. Difficulty responding calmly or logically.
3. Visible physical signs of stress, such as fidgeting or tense posture.

Once these signs are identified, both partners can take proactive steps to de-escalate the situation and prevent further flooding.

Strategies for Navigating Emotional Flooding in Relationships

To manage emotional flooding in relationships, partners and family members can work together to create an environment that fosters understanding, empathy, and effective communication.

1. Pause and Create Space for Emotional Processing
When emotional flooding occurs, taking a break can help prevent further escalation.

Practical Tip: Agree on a signal or phrase, such as "I need a moment," to pause the conversation without assigning blame.

Timeframe: Take 15-30 minutes apart to calm down, then revisit the conversation.

2. Practice Active Listening

Active listening helps reduce misunderstandings and creates a sense of being heard and validated.

Practical Tip: Focus on what your partner is saying without planning your response.

Validation: Reflect back what you hear, e.g., "It sounds like you're feeling frustrated because…"

3. Use "I" Statements

Expressing feelings using "I" statements reduces defensiveness and promotes constructive dialogue.

Example: Instead of "You always ignore me," say, "I feel hurt when I don't feel heard."

4. Offer Empathetic Support

Empathy involves understanding and acknowledging your partner's emotions without judgment.

Practical Tip: Avoid dismissing or minimizing their feelings. Instead, say, "I can see why that would be upsetting for you."

5. Establish Shared Ground Rules

Agree on boundaries and practices to handle conflicts more effectively.

Examples: No name-calling, taking breaks when needed, and ensuring both parties have time to speak.

6. Revisit Conversations When Calm

Once emotions have settled, revisit the discussion with a focus on resolution and mutual understanding.

Practical Tip: Summarize the issue and brainstorm solutions together.

Building Emotional Resilience Together

Relationships are strengthened when both partners commit to building emotional resilience and supporting each other through challenges.

1. Foster Emotional Safety

Create an environment where both partners feel safe expressing their emotions.

Practical Tip: Show patience and avoid judgment, even when emotions are intense.

2. Develop a Shared Toolbox of Coping Strategies

Collaborate to identify techniques that help each partner manage emotional flooding.

Examples: Practicing deep breathing together, engaging in mindfulness exercises, or using humor to defuse tension.

3. Seek Professional Support

Couples or family therapy can provide tools and insights for managing emotional flooding in relationships.

Benefits: A therapist can help uncover patterns, mediate conflicts, and teach effective communication skills.

Strengthening Emotional Connection

Managing emotional flooding in relationships is not just about avoiding conflict — it's about fostering deeper emotional connections. When partners or family members work together to navigate intense emotions, they build trust, empathy, and mutual understanding.

Over time, these efforts create a foundation for more fulfilling and harmonious relationships.

By recognizing the impact of emotional flooding, employing strategies to navigate it, and committing to shared growth, individuals and their loved ones can transform moments of overwhelm into opportunities for connection and resilience. In this way, emotional flooding becomes not a barrier, but a bridge to stronger relationships.

Chapter 15: Workplace Impacts

The modern workplace, with its tight deadlines, interpersonal dynamics, and high expectations, is a fertile ground for emotional flooding. When individuals experience emotional overwhelm at work, it can disrupt performance, hinder decision-making, and strain professional relationships. While employees bear the immediate impact, organizations also face productivity challenges and morale issues if emotional flooding is not effectively managed. By addressing emotional needs and fostering a supportive environment, both employees and employers can mitigate these impacts and create a healthier, more productive workplace.

Emotional Flooding in the Workplace: Causes and Manifestations

Emotional flooding in the workplace can arise from a variety of sources and often manifests in ways that affect individual and team dynamics.

Common Causes

- **High-Pressure Tasks**
  Tight deadlines and demanding projects can trigger feelings of overwhelm, especially when resources or time are limited.

- **Conflict and Poor Communication**
  Misunderstandings, power struggles, or negative interactions with colleagues or supervisors can escalate emotions.

- **Role Ambiguity or Overload**
  Unclear responsibilities or an excessive workload leave employees feeling unsupported and unable to cope.

- **Workplace Culture**
  Environments that discourage emotional expression or foster competition over collaboration can amplify stress and emotional flooding.

Common Manifestations
- **Cognitive Impairments**: Difficulty concentrating, decision paralysis, or errors in judgment.
- **Emotional Reactions**: Irritability, frustration, or feelings of helplessness.
- **Physical Symptoms**: Fatigue, headaches, or increased tension during high-stress periods.
- **Behavioral Changes**: Withdrawal, procrastination, or uncharacteristic outbursts.

Impacts on Employees and Organizations

For Employees
- **Decreased Job Satisfaction**: Persistent emotional flooding can lead to burnout, reducing overall engagement.
- **Career Stagnation**: Impaired decision-making or interpersonal conflicts may hinder professional growth.
- **Mental and Physical Health Risks**: Chronic stress from emotional flooding increases the risk of anxiety, depression, and physical health issues.

For Organizations
- **Reduced Productivity**: Emotional flooding can slow task completion and diminish work quality.
- **Higher Turnover**: Employees who feel unsupported may seek other opportunities.
- **Team Dysfunction**: Conflicts and communication breakdowns can erode team cohesion and collaboration.
- **Increased Costs**: Absenteeism, medical claims, and the expense of replacing employees contribute to organizational strain.

Strategies for Managing Emotional Flooding in the Workplace
Creating a supportive work environment requires intentional strategies that address both individual needs and organizational culture.

1. Foster Open Communication
Encourage employees to share their concerns without fear of judgment or retaliation.

Practical Tip: Train managers to practice active listening and empathy during conversations about stress or workload.

2. Promote Mindfulness Practices
Mindfulness helps employees stay present and manage stress more effectively.

Implementation:
- Offer mindfulness training sessions or guided meditation breaks.
- Create quiet spaces for reflection or relaxation during the workday.

3. Create Policies That Promote Emotional Safety
Establish workplace policies that prioritize emotional well-being.

Examples:
- Encourage work-life balance by limiting after-hours emails or meetings.
- Implement flexible work arrangements to reduce stress.
- Develop clear conflict resolution protocols.

4. Offer Access to Resources
Provide tools and support systems to help employees manage emotional challenges.

Options:
- Employee Assistance Programs (EAPs) offering counseling or therapy sessions.
- Workshops on stress management or emotional intelligence.
- Access to apps or platforms focused on mental health and resilience.

5. Encourage Peer Support
Build a culture of collaboration where employees support one another.

Implementation:
- Create peer mentoring programs or team-building activities.
- Encourage informal check-ins to foster camaraderie.

6. Develop Training for Managers
Equip leaders with the skills to recognize and address emotional flooding in their teams.

Training Focus:
- Identifying early signs of emotional flooding.
- Providing constructive feedback without escalating emotions.
- Supporting employees through high-pressure periods.

Proactive Measures for a Healthier Workplace
Preventing emotional flooding requires a proactive approach that integrates emotional wellness into the fabric of the workplace.

1. Promote a Positive Workplace Culture
Foster an inclusive, collaborative environment where employees feel valued and supported.

Practical Tip: Celebrate achievements, recognize efforts, and provide regular opportunities for professional growth.

2. Monitor Workloads
Regularly assess employee workloads to ensure tasks are manageable.

Implementation:
- Use periodic check-ins to gauge employee stress levels.
- Adjust priorities or redistribute tasks as needed.

3. Encourage Regular Breaks
Breaks allow employees to recharge and return to tasks with renewed focus.

Practical Tip: Implement policies that encourage stepping away, such as scheduled break times or walking meetings.

4. Provide Continuous Learning Opportunities
Equip employees with emotional regulation skills.

Options:
- Workshops on topics like mindfulness, conflict resolution, and emotional intelligence.
- Online courses or resources employees can access at their convenience.

Building Resilience and Productivity
A workplace that acknowledges and addresses emotional flooding fosters not only healthier employees but also stronger teams and improved outcomes. By implementing strategies that prioritize emotional well-being, organizations can create an environment where employees feel empowered to manage stress, communicate effectively, and thrive under pressure.

Investing in emotional wellness isn't just an act of compassion—it's a strategic decision that drives long-term success. When employees and employers collaborate to build a supportive workplace, they unlock the potential for greater resilience, connection, and productivity across all levels of the organization.

Chapter 16: Emotional Flooding in Parenting

Parenting is one of life's most rewarding yet challenging roles. It involves navigating not only your own emotions but also those of your children, who are still learning how to process and express what they feel. Emotional flooding can arise in both parents and children, disrupting communication and escalating stress within the family. Understanding how to recognize and address emotional flooding is key to fostering a healthy, resilient household.

Recognizing Emotional Flooding in Children and Teens
Children and teens experience emotional flooding differently than adults. They may not have the language or self-awareness to articulate their feelings, often expressing them through behaviors instead.

Signs of Emotional Flooding in Children
- **Acting Out**: Tantrums, yelling, hitting, or other forms of aggression may signal emotional overwhelm.
- **Withdrawal**: Shutting down, avoiding eye contact, or refusing to engage can indicate internalized distress.
- **Physical Symptoms**: Complaints of stomachaches, headaches, or feeling sick may stem from emotional stress.
- **Increased Sensitivity**: Overreacting to minor frustrations or setbacks.

Signs of Emotional Flooding in Teens
- **Mood Swings**: Sudden shifts from anger to sadness or irritability to withdrawal.
- **Risky Behaviors**: Experimenting with substances, skipping responsibilities, or engaging in dangerous activities as a form of emotional release.
- **Isolation**: Spending excessive time alone or disengaging from family and friends.
- **Difficulty Concentrating**: Struggling with schoolwork or routine tasks due to overwhelming emotions.

How Parenting Style Impacts Emotional Flooding

Parental responses to emotional flooding play a significant role in shaping how children learn to manage their emotions.

Supportive Parenting
- Encourages open communication about emotions.
- Models healthy coping mechanisms.
- Provides a sense of safety and stability.

Reactive Parenting
- Responds to children's emotions with frustration, anger, or dismissal.
- Escalates emotional flooding by invalidating or intensifying feelings.
- Creates a cycle of miscommunication and heightened emotions.

Managing Emotional Flooding in Yourself as a Parent

Parenting while emotionally flooded can lead to reactive decisions and strained relationships. It's essential to manage your emotions first before addressing your child's needs.

1. Pause Before Reacting
- Take a few deep breaths or count to ten before responding to your child's behavior.
- If needed, step away momentarily to regain composure.

2. Acknowledge Your Feelings
- Identify what you're feeling and why. Naming your emotions can help diffuse their intensity.

    Example: "I'm feeling frustrated because this is the third time, I've asked for the dishes to be done."

3. Practice Self-Compassion
- Remind yourself that it's okay to feel overwhelmed and that parenting is a learning process.
- Avoid self-blame, focusing instead on what you can do to improve the situation.

4. Use Grounding Techniques
- Engage in a quick mindfulness exercise, such as focusing on your breath or a physical sensation, to calm your nervous system.

Helping Your Child Navigate Emotional Flooding
When children are emotionally flooded, they need guidance and support to process their feelings. Here's how parents can help:

1. Create a Safe Space for Emotional Expression
Encourage your child to share their feelings without fear of judgment or punishment.

> **Example**: "It's okay to feel angry or upset. Let's talk about what's bothering you."

2. Validate Their Emotions
Acknowledge what they're feeling without minimizing or dismissing it.

> **Example**: "I can see you're really frustrated right now. That's understandable."

3. Teach Coping Strategies
Introduce age-appropriate techniques to help children manage overwhelm:

> **Breathing Exercises**: Teach deep belly breathing or box breathing to calm their body.
> **Mindfulness Activities**: Encourage them to focus on the present moment, such as naming five things they can see or hear.
> **Physical Outlets**: Suggest physical activities like running, dancing, or squeezing a stress ball to release pent-up energy.

4. Offer Comfort and Reassurance

Provide physical and emotional comfort to help them feel secure.

Example: A warm hug or reassuring words like, "I'm here to help you through this."

Building Emotional Resilience Within the Family

Fostering emotional resilience equips children with lifelong skills for managing stress and overwhelm. It also strengthens the family unit, creating a more harmonious environment.

1. Model Healthy Emotional Regulation

Demonstrate how to manage your emotions constructively so your children can learn by example.

Example: "I'm feeling a little overwhelmed, so I'm going to take a few deep breaths before we keep talking."

2. Establish Predictable Routines

Consistent routines provide children with a sense of stability, reducing anxiety and emotional flooding.

Example: Regular family meals, bedtime routines, or weekly check-ins.

3. Encourage Open Communication

Make it a habit to talk about emotions as a family.

Practical Tip: Use dinnertime or a weekly family meeting to discuss highs and lows from the week.

4. Celebrate Progress

Acknowledge your child's efforts to manage their emotions and your own improvements as a parent.

Example: "I noticed how you used your breathing exercise when you got upset earlier. Great job!"

The Long-Term Impact of Emotional Resilience
Children who learn to navigate emotional flooding with
support and guidance grow into adults with strong emotional
regulation skills. By creating a safe, supportive environment
and modeling healthy behaviors, parents can help their children
develop tools to manage stress and overwhelm throughout their
lives.

Parenting through emotional flooding is not about perfection—
it's about showing up with patience, understanding, and a
commitment to growth. When parents and children work
together to navigate intense emotions, they strengthen their
bond and lay the foundation for a resilient, emotionally healthy
family.

Part 6 - Thriving Beyond Emotional Flooding

Chapter 17: Healing from Past Flooding Experiences - Healing from emotional flooding requires addressing unresolved trauma and understanding its lingering effects on emotional and mental health. Confronting these past experiences allows individuals to process their emotions and release the weight of old wounds. Practicing forgiveness — whether for oneself or others — combined with self-compassion, fosters emotional healing and opens the door to moving forward with greater clarity and strength.

Chapter 18: Building a Supportive Network - A strong support system is vital for emotional health and resilience. Surrounding oneself with understanding, trustworthy individuals creates a sense of safety during challenging times. Communicating needs effectively to loved ones strengthens these connections and ensures that support is available when it's needed most. By fostering open, honest relationships, individuals can navigate emotional flooding with the help of a reliable and empathetic network.

Chapter 19: Living with Emotional Awareness - Living beyond emotional flooding involves embracing emotions as a strength rather than a burden. Developing emotional awareness and intelligence equips individuals to manage their feelings constructively, improving their relationships and overall well-being. This chapter emphasizes the importance of emotional self-awareness, self-regulation, and the pursuit of long-term mental health. Harnessing emotions as tools for growth and understanding allows individuals to thrive with resilience and confidence.

This final section focuses on overcoming the lingering effects of emotional flooding, cultivating a supportive community, and transforming emotional awareness into a source of strength. It provides a roadmap for living a more balanced and emotionally intelligent life.

Chapter 17: Healing from Past Flooding Experiences

Emotional flooding, especially when tied to unresolved trauma, can leave a lasting impact on mental and emotional well-being. Past flooding experiences often carry unresolved pain, limiting personal growth and creating patterns of reactivity in the present. Healing from these experiences involves confronting old wounds, processing lingering emotions, and developing tools for moving forward with clarity and strength.

The Lingering Effects of Past Flooding Experiences
When emotional flooding is left unaddressed, its effects can manifest in various ways, influencing daily life and relationships.

Emotional Impact
- Persistent feelings of fear, shame, or guilt tied to past events.
- Difficulty trusting others or forming close relationships due to unresolved emotional pain.
- Low self-esteem or self-worth stemming from past flooding episodes.

Cognitive Impact
1. Negative thought patterns, such as self-blame or catastrophizing.
2. Difficulty focusing or making decisions when emotions are triggered.
3. Avoidance of situations that might evoke similar overwhelming emotions.

Physical Impact
- Chronic stress symptoms, such as fatigue, headaches, or muscle tension.
- Increased susceptibility to anxiety or depression.
- A hyperactive fight-or-flight response, even in non-threatening situations.

Understanding these lingering effects is the first step in breaking free from their grip and reclaiming emotional stability.

Confronting Past Flooding Experiences
Healing begins with acknowledging and processing past flooding episodes. Confronting these experiences allows individuals to release their hold on the present.

Recognize the Source of Flooding
Reflect on significant moments when emotional flooding occurred.

> **Practical Tip**: Use journaling to explore these events. Write down what happened, how you felt, and how it affected you.

Identify patterns, such as recurring triggers or similar emotional responses.

Accept Your Emotions
Allow yourself to feel the emotions tied to past experiences without judgment.

> **Mantra**: "It's okay to feel this way. My emotions are valid."

> Recognize that emotions are a natural response to difficult experiences and not a sign of weakness.

Seek Professional Guidance
Therapy can provide a safe space to explore past flooding experiences and their impact.

Options:
- Trauma-focused therapy to address unresolved wounds.
- Cognitive Behavioral Therapy (CBT) to reframe negative thought patterns.
- Eye Movement Desensitization and Reprocessing (EMDR) for processing traumatic memories.

Practicing Forgiveness and Self-Compassion

Forgiveness and self-compassion are powerful tools for releasing the weight of past flooding experiences and fostering emotional healing.

1. Forgiveness of Others

Forgiving those who may have contributed to your emotional flooding does not condone their actions but frees you from carrying resentment.

> **Practical Tip**: Write a letter to the person (even if you never send it) expressing your feelings and your decision to release the pain.

2. Forgiveness of Yourself

Let go of self-blame for how you reacted during past flooding episodes.

> **Mantra**: "I did the best I could with what I knew at the time."
> - Acknowledge your growth and resilience in learning from these experiences.

3. Cultivate Self-Compassion

Treat yourself with kindness as you navigate the healing process.

> **Practical Tip**: Practice daily affirmations, such as, "I am worthy of healing and peace."

Releasing the Weight of Old Wounds

Healing from past flooding experiences involves letting go of the emotional baggage tied to those moments. This process creates space for growth and clarity.

1. Engage in Emotional Release Practices

Use techniques to safely release pent-up emotions:

- **Journaling**: Write freely about your feelings, allowing yourself to process and release them.
- **Creative Outlets**: Express emotions through art, music, or movement.
- **Somatic Practices**: Engage in body-focused practices, such as yoga or breathwork, to release stored tension.

2. Reframe Your Narrative

Shift how you view past experiences to focus on resilience and growth.

Example: Instead of "I failed during that time," try, "I learned valuable lessons that have made me stronger."

3. Establish New Emotional Patterns

Develop habits that prevent old wounds from resurfacing in unhelpful ways:

- Set healthy boundaries with people or situations that may trigger past flooding.
- Practice mindfulness to remain present and grounded during emotional challenges.

Moving Forward with Clarity and Strength

Healing from past emotional flooding doesn't mean erasing the memory—it means transforming how it shapes your present and future.

1. Celebrate Small Wins

Acknowledge progress, even if it feels small.

Example: Recognize moments when you respond to a trigger with calm instead of reactivity.

2. Build a Support System

Surround yourself with people who uplift and support your healing journey.

Practical Tip: Share your goals for emotional growth with trusted friends or family members.

3. Focus on Emotional Resilience
Strengthen your ability to handle future emotional challenges: Practice grounding techniques and breathing exercises regularly.

Engage in activities that bring joy and promote relaxation.

The Power of Healing
Healing from emotional flooding is a journey of self-discovery, resilience, and empowerment. By confronting past experiences, practicing forgiveness, and cultivating self-compassion, individuals can release the weight of old wounds and reclaim control over their emotional lives.

This process not only brings greater peace and clarity but also strengthens the foundation for healthier relationships, improved mental health, and a more fulfilling life. Emotional flooding, once a source of overwhelm, becomes a stepping stone toward growth and transformation.

Chapter 18: Building a Supportive Network

No one should have to face emotional flooding or its challenges alone. A supportive network of trustworthy and understanding individuals can be a powerful source of strength during difficult times. Such relationships foster a sense of safety, provide perspective, and offer comfort when emotions feel overwhelming. By intentionally cultivating a strong support system and learning how to communicate needs effectively, individuals can navigate emotional flooding with greater confidence and resilience.

The Importance of a Supportive Network
A reliable support system can significantly enhance emotional well-being and resilience by providing:

1. Emotional Safety
- Feeling understood and accepted by others reduces the intensity of emotional flooding and creates a space for vulnerability.

2. Perspective
- Trusted individuals can offer insights or reassurance that help reframe challenges and reduce emotional overwhelm.

3. Practical Assistance
- A strong network can provide tangible support, such as help with tasks, guidance, or simply being present during tough times.

4. Connection
- Positive relationships counteract feelings of isolation, reinforcing the idea that you are not alone in your struggles.

Identifying Supportive Individuals
Not all relationships are equally supportive. It's important to identify people who contribute positively to your emotional health.

Characteristics of a Supportive Person
- **Empathy**: They listen without judgment and validate your feelings.
- **Reliability**: They show up consistently when you need them.
- **Trustworthiness**: They respect your privacy and maintain confidentiality.
- **Positivity**: They encourage and uplift you without dismissing your challenges.

Types of Supportive Relationships
- **Family**: Relatives who share a close bond and a history of mutual care.
- **Friends**: Trusted peers who offer companionship and understanding.
- **Community Members**: Neighbors, religious groups, or support groups that share common values or experiences.
- **Professionals**: Therapists, counselors, or coaches who provide expert guidance and a neutral perspective.

Strengthening Existing Relationships
Even strong relationships require effort and intentionality to deepen their supportive potential.

1. Open Communication
Be honest about your feelings and needs to foster mutual understanding.

> **Example**: "I've been feeling really overwhelmed lately, and it would help if we could talk about it."

2. Practice Active Listening
Show genuine interest in others' experiences, which strengthens the bond of reciprocity.

Tip: Reflect back what the other person says to show you're engaged, e.g., "It sounds like that's been really challenging for you."

3. Set Boundaries
Protect your emotional health by clarifying what you need in the relationship.

Example: "I appreciate your advice, but right now, I just need someone to listen."

4. Express Gratitude
Acknowledge and thank others for their support to reinforce positive interactions.

Example: "I'm so grateful for how you've been there for me. It means a lot."

Communicating Your Needs Effectively
To receive the support you need, it's crucial to communicate your needs clearly and assertively.

1. Be Specific
Clearly articulate what kind of support you're seeking.

Example: "Can you help me brainstorm solutions?" or "Can we set aside time to talk this weekend?"

2. Use "I" Statements
Frame requests in a way that focuses on your feelings and needs rather than placing blame.

Example: "I feel overwhelmed and could use some help organizing my thoughts."

3. Be Open to Feedback
Allow space for the other person to share their perspective or limitations.

Example: "If there's anything you need from me to make this easier, please let me know."

4. Respect Their Boundaries
Understand that even supportive individuals may have their own limits.

Example: "I understand if you're busy right now — just let me know when you're available."

Expanding Your Support System
If your current network feels limited, consider ways to expand and diversify it.

1. Join Support Groups
Look for groups tailored to your experiences, such as mental health support groups or parenting forums.

Benefit: Sharing with others who understand your challenges fosters connection and reduces isolation.

2. Engage in Community Activities
Volunteer, join clubs, or attend community events to meet like-minded individuals.

Benefit: Building connections in shared spaces strengthens your sense of belonging.

3. Seek Professional Support
Therapists or counselors can become invaluable members of your support system, offering tools and insights to navigate emotional flooding.

Fostering a Supportive Environment
Creating a supportive network also involves cultivating an environment that encourages open dialogue and emotional safety.

1. Lead by Example

Model healthy communication and emotional regulation to inspire similar behavior in others.

2. Encourage Mutual Support
Create opportunities for shared vulnerability by offering support to others in return.

> **Example**: "I know you've been stressed too—how can I help you?"

3. Build a Culture of Openness
Normalize discussions about emotions and challenges within your circle.

> **Tip**: Start conversations about emotional health to encourage others to do the same.

Navigating Emotional Flooding Together
A supportive network doesn't just help in times of emotional flooding—it equips you with tools to face challenges more effectively. By fostering open, honest relationships and communicating your needs clearly, you create a foundation of trust and empathy that strengthens your resilience.

Remember, building and maintaining a supportive network takes time and effort, but the rewards are immeasurable. With the right people by your side, you can face emotional flooding with confidence, knowing you are supported, understood, and never truly alone.

Chapter 19: Living with Emotional Awareness

Living with emotional awareness means embracing emotions as a valuable part of life, rather than viewing them as a burden. By developing emotional intelligence and self-awareness, individuals can better understand their feelings, respond constructively, and improve their relationships and overall well-being. Emotional awareness is not about eliminating challenges or difficult emotions—it's about learning to harness them as tools for growth, resilience, and personal empowerment.

What Is Emotional Awareness?
Emotional awareness is the ability to recognize, understand, and make sense of your own emotions and those of others. It is the foundation of emotional intelligence, which involves using this awareness to navigate life's challenges effectively.

Core Components of Emotional Awareness
Emotional Self-Awareness
- Recognizing and understanding your own emotions as they arise.
- Acknowledging the connections between your feelings, thoughts, and behaviors.

Self-Regulation
- Managing and expressing emotions in a way that is constructive and balanced.
- Avoiding impulsive reactions and maintaining control during stressful situations.

Empathy
- Understanding and validating the emotions of others.
- Building deeper connections through compassionate responses.

The Benefits of Living with Emotional Awareness

Embracing emotional awareness enhances every aspect of life, from personal growth to interpersonal relationships and overall mental health.

1. Improved Emotional Resilience

Understanding your emotions allows you to respond calmly and effectively to challenges.

> **Example**: Recognizing the signs of emotional flooding and using grounding techniques to regain control.

2. Stronger Relationships

Emotional awareness fosters better communication and empathy, strengthening bonds with others.

> **Example**: Listening actively and validating a partner's feelings during a disagreement.

3. Enhanced Mental Health

Acknowledging and processing emotions reduces the risk of emotional suppression, which can lead to stress or anxiety.

> **Example**: Journaling or discussing feelings with a trusted friend or therapist.

4. Greater Self-Empowerment

Recognizing and honoring your emotions helps you make more aligned decisions and set healthy boundaries.

> **Example**: Declining a commitment when you feel emotionally stretched.

Developing Emotional Awareness

Living with emotional awareness is a skill that can be cultivated through intentional practice and reflection.

1. Practice Emotional Self-Awareness
Identify Your Emotions: Take time to label your emotions throughout the day.

> **Tip**: Use a feelings chart or app to track your emotions and identify patterns.

Reflect on Triggers: Consider what causes certain emotional responses and why.

> **Example**: "I feel anxious during team meetings because I'm afraid of being judged."

2. Build Emotional Vocabulary
Expand your emotional vocabulary to describe feelings more precisely.

> **Examples**: Replace "I'm upset" with "I feel disappointed" or "I feel overwhelmed."

3. Tune Into Your Body
Recognize how emotions manifest physically.

> **Example**: A racing heart may indicate anxiety, while clenched fists could signal anger.

4. Practice Mindfulness
Mindfulness helps you observe your emotions without judgment.

> **Practical Exercise**: Spend 5 minutes focusing on your breath and noticing any emotions that arise.

Strengthening Self-Regulation
Self-regulation involves responding to emotions in a way that aligns with your values and long-term goals.

1. Create a Pause
Give yourself time to respond rather than reacting impulsively.

Tip: Count to ten or take a few deep breaths before responding during heated moments.

2. Reframe Negative Thoughts
Challenge and reframe unhelpful thought patterns to reduce emotional intensity.

> **Example**: Replace "I always mess up" with "I made a mistake, but I'm learning."

3. Set Healthy Boundaries
Protect your emotional well-being by setting limits with others.

> **Example**: "I need some time to think before we continue this conversation."

4. Develop Healthy Outlets
Channel emotions constructively through creative, physical, or reflective activities.

> **Examples**: Painting, exercising, or journaling about your feelings.

Cultivating Emotional Awareness in Relationships
Emotional awareness extends beyond yourself — it also involves understanding and responding to others' emotions.

1. Practice Active Listening
Give others your full attention and validate their emotions without jumping to solutions.

> **Example**: "It sounds like you're feeling frustrated. Do you want to talk more about it?"

2. Show Empathy
Put yourself in others' shoes to better understand their perspectives.

Example: "I can see why that would upset you. I'd feel the same way."

3. Manage Conflicts Constructively
Approach disagreements with curiosity rather than defensiveness.

Tip: Focus on finding solutions rather than assigning blame.

Long-Term Practices for Emotional Awareness
Living with emotional awareness is a lifelong practice that evolves over time.

1. Regular Self-Reflection
Set aside time to reflect on your emotions and how you handled them.

Prompt: "What emotions did I experience today? How did I respond, and what could I improve?"

2. Seek Feedback
Ask trusted friends, family, or colleagues for insights into your emotional interactions.

Example: "How do you feel I handle difficult conversations?"

3. Prioritize Mental Health
Invest in your emotional well-being through therapy, meditation, or support groups.

4. Celebrate Progress
Acknowledge and celebrate your growth in emotional awareness and regulation.

Example: "I stayed calm during that conflict, and I'm proud of how I handled it."

Thriving with Resilience and Confidence

Living with emotional awareness transforms how you navigate life's challenges and relationships. It equips you to handle emotions constructively, fostering resilience, improving your connections with others, and promoting a deeper understanding of yourself.

Emotions, when embraced as tools for growth, become a source of strength rather than a burden. By cultivating emotional awareness, you can move through life with clarity, confidence, and an unshakable sense of empowerment, no matter what comes your way.

Bonus Chapter

Emotional Flooding and Compulsive Behaviors – A Comprehensive Perspective

Emotional flooding and compulsive behaviors are often interconnected in a complex relationship of emotional regulation and coping. Compulsive behaviors—such as overeating, substance use, shopping, or repetitive rituals—can arise as a response to emotional flooding, providing temporary relief but often leading to long-term challenges. Understanding this link offers a path to healthier coping mechanisms and deeper emotional healing.

The Connection Between Emotional Flooding and Compulsive Behaviors

1. Emotional Overload as a Trigger
- Emotional flooding overwhelms the brain's capacity to process emotions, activating the fight, flight, or freeze response.
- Compulsive behaviors can act as a *flight mechanism*, allowing individuals to escape or numb their emotional distress.

2. The Temporary Relief Loop
- Compulsive behaviors provide a short-term sense of control or relief from overwhelming emotions.

> **Example**: A person feeling emotionally flooded might binge eat to soothe themselves, leading to a temporary sense of calm.

- Over time, this relief reinforces the behavior, creating a cycle that is difficult to break.

3. Avoidance of Underlying Issues
Compulsive behaviors distract from the underlying emotions or triggers of emotional flooding.

Example: Instead of addressing feelings of inadequacy after a conflict, someone might compulsively shop to create a false sense of empowerment or happiness.

Types of Compulsive Behaviors Linked to Emotional Flooding

1. Substance Use
- Alcohol, drugs, or other substances may be used to numb the emotional intensity of flooding.
- This can lead to dependency, masking the root cause of emotional distress.

2. Emotional Eating
- Food provides a sensory and emotional distraction, often triggering the brain's reward centers.
- Over time, this can lead to unhealthy eating patterns or disordered eating.

3. Overspending or Shopping Addiction
- Buying items can create a fleeting sense of control or fulfillment, but the emotional flooding often resurfaces once the initial high subsides.

4. Ritualistic Behaviors
- Repetitive actions, such as excessive cleaning or checking, may provide a false sense of security or order in the face of emotional chaos.

5. Technology and Screen Addiction
- Excessive use of social media, gaming, or streaming may serve as a way to escape the discomfort of emotional flooding.

The Science Behind the Cycle

1. The Role of the Brain
- Emotional flooding activates the amygdala, the brain's emotional center, which can overpower the prefrontal cortex, responsible for logical thinking and impulse control.
- Compulsive behaviors stimulate dopamine release, temporarily counteracting the distress signals from the amygdala.

2. The Impact of Stress Hormones
- During emotional flooding, elevated cortisol levels increase the urge to seek comfort or distraction, making compulsive behaviors more appealing.

3. The Habit Loop
- Emotional flooding → Compulsive behavior → Temporary relief → Emotional flooding returns → Compulsive behavior (and the cycle repeats).

Breaking the Cycle: Addressing Emotional Flooding and Compulsive Behaviors

1. Recognize the Pattern
Step 1: Identify when emotional flooding precedes compulsive behavior.

> **Example**: "I notice that I binge-eat after I have a stressful conversation at work."

Step 2: Journal your emotions and actions to uncover triggers and patterns.

2. Build Emotional Awareness
Use mindfulness to observe emotions without judgment, creating space between the feeling and the compulsion.

Exercise: Sit with your emotions for 1–2 minutes, describing them in detail without acting on them.

3. Develop Alternative Coping Strategies
Replace compulsive behaviors with healthier outlets:

> **For stress eating**: Practice deep breathing or drink a glass of water before eating.
> **For overspending**: Pause and reflect on the necessity of a purchase; create a waiting period before buying.

4. Strengthen Emotional Regulation
Incorporate emotional regulation techniques such as:

> **Grounding exercises**: Focus on sensory experiences to stay present.
> **Cognitive reframing**: Shift from catastrophic thinking to a more balanced perspective.

5. Address the Underlying Triggers
Work with a therapist to explore the root causes of emotional flooding and compulsive behaviors, such as unresolved trauma, unmet emotional needs, or stressors.

Long-Term Strategies for Healing
1. Develop a Support System
Share your struggles with trusted friends, family, or support groups to create accountability and reduce isolation.

2. Practice Self-Compassion
Avoid self-judgment for experiencing emotional flooding or engaging in compulsive behaviors.

> **Mantra**: "I am doing my best to learn and grow."

3. Use Gradual Exposure
Gradually expose yourself to emotional triggers while practicing healthier responses.

Example: Face small, manageable stressors and practice breathing exercises to stay calm.

4. Consider Professional Help
Therapy approaches such as:

CBT: Helps identify and reframe negative thought patterns linked to compulsive behaviors.
DBT: Teaches skills for emotional regulation, distress tolerance, and mindfulness.

Thriving Beyond Emotional Flooding and Compulsions
Healing from the cycle of emotional flooding and compulsive behaviors requires patience and persistence. By understanding the connection between emotions and actions, developing healthier coping strategies, and addressing the root causes of distress, individuals can reclaim control over their emotional lives.

Emotions, when managed constructively, become a tool for growth rather than a trigger for avoidance. Living with emotional awareness and intention allows individuals to break free from the cycle of compulsive behaviors, building resilience and thriving in all areas of life.

CONCLUSION

A Path Toward Emotional Awareness and Resilience

Emotional flooding is a universal experience, one that affects people across all ages, genders, and backgrounds. While its intensity can be overwhelming, understanding it is the first step in regaining control and creating a healthier relationship with your emotions. This book has aimed to demystify emotional flooding, providing insights into its causes, manifestations, and the profound impact it has on mental health and relationships.

The Journey We've Taken

From understanding the anatomy of emotional flooding and its triggers to exploring its long-term effects, we've uncovered the many facets of this phenomenon. We've examined its links to mental health conditions, its role in interpersonal conflicts, and its unique manifestations across various life stages. Most importantly, we've explored tools and strategies to manage emotional flooding, from immediate coping techniques to preventative measures, professional support, and building emotional resilience.

In the context of relationships, parenting, and the workplace, we've seen how emotional flooding doesn't just affect individuals—it also shapes the dynamics of the communities we belong to. We've also touched on the importance of healing from past flooding experiences, cultivating supportive networks, and living with emotional awareness as a way to thrive.

Moving Beyond Emotional Flooding

The journey toward emotional awareness and resilience doesn't end here. This book is just the beginning—a foundation for deeper learning and personal growth. Emotional flooding is not something to be feared or suppressed; it's an opportunity to connect with yourself, to better understand your needs, and to use emotions as a tool for growth and connection.

By embracing the practices and insights shared here, you can:
- Recognize and address emotional flooding when it arises.
- Build stronger relationships with those around you through empathy and understanding.
- Foster a life of emotional balance, self-awareness, and long-term mental health.

A Call to Action
Knowledge is the seed of transformation. Once you understand emotional flooding, you can't "un-know" it. You have the power to cultivate this awareness into meaningful action—whether it's making small daily changes, seeking support when needed, or simply extending compassion to yourself and others.

The road to emotional resilience may not always be easy, but it is one worth traveling. With each step you take, you're not only improving your own well-being but also contributing to a more understanding and emotionally aware world. Let this knowledge be your guide as you move forward with clarity, confidence, and hope.

Here's to living with emotional awareness and thriving beyond emotional flooding.

RESOURCE LIST

These resources aim to support readers in understanding, managing, and healing from emotional flooding, while fostering long-term emotional health.

Books
1. *The Body Keeps the Score* by Bessel van der Kolk - Explores the connection between trauma and the body, providing insights into how emotional flooding can stem from unresolved trauma.
2. *Emotional Intelligence 2.0* by Travis Bradberry and Jean Greaves - Offers practical strategies for improving emotional awareness and regulation.
3. *Mindfulness for Beginners* by Jon Kabat-Zinn - A guide to mindfulness practices that can help manage emotional flooding.
4. *Nonviolent Communication: A Language of Life* by Marshall B. Rosenberg - Teaches effective communication strategies to manage emotions during conflicts.
5. *Rising Strong* by Brené Brown - Discusses how to navigate emotions and rise stronger after experiencing setbacks.

Online Courses
1. **Mindfulness-Based Stress Reduction (MBSR)**
   - Offered by various platforms like UMass Online and Insight Timer.
   - Teaches mindfulness techniques to handle emotional overwhelm.
2. **The Science of Well-Being** (Yale University via Coursera)
   - Free course focusing on habits and strategies for improving mental health and emotional regulation.
3. **Dialectical Behavior Therapy (DBT) Skills Training**
   - Available through platforms like DBT Path and Psychology Tools.

Mobile Apps

1. **Calm** - Offers guided meditations, breathing exercises, and relaxation techniques to reduce stress and manage emotional flooding.
2. **Headspace** - Provides mindfulness and emotional regulation exercises suitable for all levels.
3. **Moodpath** - A mental health tracking app that helps users identify patterns in their emotional experiences.
4. **Stop, Breathe & Think** - Focuses on mindfulness and emotional awareness through short, targeted exercises.
5. **Woebot** - An AI-based chatbot that helps users work through emotions using CBT principles.

Worksheets and Printables

1. **Emotional Regulation Worksheets**
   - Available on Therapist Aid, focusing on identifying triggers and managing emotions.
2. **Mindfulness Exercises**
   - Printable mindfulness and grounding activities from Positive Psychology.
3. **DBT Skills Handouts**
   - Free resources from DBT Skills Training Manual.

Support Groups

1. **National Alliance on Mental Illness (NAMI)**
   - Offers free peer-led support groups for individuals experiencing emotional challenges. Find a support group.
2. **Emotions Anonymous**
   - A 12-step program for individuals struggling with overwhelming emotions. Learn more.
3. **Online Communities**
   - Join forums like Reddit's r/mentalhealth or PsychCentral's Community for peer support.

Podcasts
1. **Unlocking Us with Brené Brown**
   - Focuses on vulnerability, resilience, and emotional growth.
2. **The Happiness Lab** with Dr. Laurie Santos
   - Discusses science-based strategies for improving emotional well-being.
3. **The Calm Collective**
   - Explores mindfulness, grief, and emotional processing.
4. **Therapy Chat**
   - Covers topics related to emotional health, relationships, and trauma.
5. **Mindfulness for Beginners Podcast**
   - Short, actionable mindfulness tips to manage emotions.

Videos and Documentaries
1. **TED Talks**
   - *"The Power of Vulnerability"* by Brené Brown
   - *"How to Make Stress Your Friend"* by Kelly McGonigal
   - *"What Trauma Taught Me About Resilience"* by Charles Hunt
2. **Documentaries**
   - *Heal* (Netflix): Explores the mind-body connection in emotional and physical healing.
   - *The Mind, Explained* (Netflix): Offers insights into how emotions work.

Professional Organizations
1. **American Psychological Association (APA)**
   - Provides resources and tools for emotional health. Visit APA.
2. **BetterHelp**
   - Access to licensed therapists for online counseling. Visit BetterHelp.
3. **Psychology Today**

- A directory of therapists and counselors specializing in emotional regulation. Find a Therapist.

Breathing and Relaxation Tools
1. **YouTube Channels**
   - *Yoga with Adriene*: Free yoga videos for stress relief and emotional regulation.
   - *Calm*: Guided breathing exercises and nature-inspired relaxation videos.
2. **Biofeedback Devices**
   - **HeartMath Inner Balance**: Helps monitor stress and practice emotional self-regulation.
   - **Muse Headband**: Guides meditation using real-time feedback.

Hotlines and Crisis Resources
1. **National Suicide Prevention Lifeline (USA)**
   - Call 988 for free, confidential support 24/7.
2. **Crisis Text Line**
   - Text HOME to 741741 for support via text in the U.S. and Canada.
3. **Mental Health Helpline by Country**
   - A global directory of mental health hotlines: Check Here.

These resources can serve as a valuable extension to the book on emotional flooding, offering readers practical tools, support, and avenues for deeper exploration and healing.

NOTES

Other Titles Available

- Finding Hope in God's Word as Survivors of Childhood Trauma: Therapeutic Devotional

- Therapeutic Journal Prompts: 10 Subjects, Over 300 Prompts

- 90 Days - Developing a Deeper Relationship with God

- You Don't Know What You Don't Know...: (Series with Multiple Titles)

- The Worth Within: 10 Practices to Transform Your Life and Reclaim Your Confidence

- Decision Making with God in Mind: A process in helping alleviate anxiety and hopelessness

- Lights in the Darkness - Reparenting Yourself after Childhood Trauma

- It's Not About Blame but Understanding: Healing the Hurts of the Past

- Finding Freedom in Love: Untangling Mother's Expectations and God's Grace

- Parenting Teens and Young Adults - Workbook: (...reducing the likelihood of failure to launch)

Printed in Dunstable, United Kingdom

66639676R00070